BREADFRUIT
AGROFORESTRY
GUIDE

patagonia

PROVISIONS®

Department
of Agriculture
STATE OF HAWAII

AGROFORESTRY NET
TREES OF LIFE, TREES FOR LIFE

Breadfruit Agroforestry Guide:
Planning and implementation of regenerative organic methods

By Craig R. Elevitch and Diane Ragone

© 2018 Craig R. Elevitch and Diane Ragone

Hand-drawn illustrations by Christi A. Sobel

ISBN: 978-1-939618-07-8
Library of Congress Control Number: 2018902489

Printed in USA

First edition May 2018

Recommended citation

Elevitch, C.R., and D. Ragone. 2018. *Breadfruit Agroforestry Guide: Planning and implementation of regenerative organic methods.* Breadfruit Institute of the National Tropical Botanical Garden, Kalaheo, Hawaii and Permanent Agriculture Resources, Holualoa, Hawaii. www.ntbg.org/breadfruit and www. agroforestry.net.

Sponsors

This publication was produced with funds from **Patagonia Provisions®** and the **State of Hawai'i Department of Agriculture**. Additional support was received from **Western Sustainable Agriculture Research and Education** and the **Kauai County Office of Economic Development**. Any opinions, findings, conclusions, or recommendations expressed in this publication are those of the authors and do not necessarily reflect the view of the sponsors or their affiliates.

Disclaimers

Publishers

Breadfruit Institute
National Tropical Botanical Garden
3530 Papalina Road
Kalaheo, Kauai, Hawaii USA 96741
Email: breadfruitinstitute@ntbg.org
Web: www.ntbg.org/breadfruit

Permanent Agriculture Resources
P.O. Box 428
Holualoa, Hawaii USA 96725
Email: editor@agroforestry.net
Web: www.agroforestry.net

CONTENTS

ACKNOWLEDGMENTS

This publication builds upon the work of numerous colleagues, farmers, and friends of the breadfruit tree. It grows from knowledge first cultivated by countless farmers of the Pacific Islands, those who not only mastered the art of growing biodiverse food forests but who also selected and propagated the cultivars of breadfruit that were passed down to present day through countless generations. We humbly thank those who have laid the path forward with unparalleled generosity of spirit.

This guide also builds upon the pioneering resources of colleagues who have written and taught about breadfruit production in recent years including Andrew McGregor, Laura Roberts-Nkrumah, Seymour Webster, and Nature's Way Cooperative, among many others. We are grateful to Birgit Cameron, Kai Hinson, Michael Besancon, and Roger Still for their guidance and advice. We are especially grateful for Dan Rudoy's guidance on project development and innovative application of organic agricultural techniques to breadfruit cultivation. Foundational research on breadfruit cultivars and nutrition by Nyree Zerega, Susan Murch, Carmen Nochera, and Max Jones also influenced this work on many levels. Juliana Prater provided support services that helped make this publication possible.

The imprint of Jim Wiseman's deep and long-standing commitment to breadfruit can be felt throughout this publication, accented by his breadfruit cultivar photos. Christi A. Sobel created a range of delightful hand-drawn illustrations for this guide while also remaining faithful to botanical accuracy. For their influence on this publication, we also thank Heidi Bornhorst (pruning and tree care), Ian Cole (pruning), Scot Nelson (pests and diseases of monocultures), and Niki Mazaroli (organic certification). For photo opportunities, we are indebted to Chef Sam Choy, John Cadman, ChoiceMART, Cindy Walsh, Duke Morgan, the Faleofa 'Ohana, and breadfruit producers of Samoa, Fiji, Pohnpei, and Hawaii. We also thank the many volunteers and staff of NTBG

who made the breadfruit agroforestry conversion at McBryde Garden successful, including the previous demonstration manager Paul Massey and the current manager Noel Dickinson.

We greatly appreciate the numerous thoughtful comments on and corrections to the manuscript from a wealth of perspectives and regions provided by reviewers Jim Currie, Noel Dickinson, Roger Leakey, Neil Logan, Seei Molimau-Samasoni, Niki Mazaroli, Ted Radovich, Mary Taylor, Lex Thomson, and Nat Tuivavalagi.

Craig extends his deepest personal appreciation for the generous lessons related to breadfruit agroforestry from Paapalii Dr. Failautusi Avegalio, Kumu M. Kalani Souza, Aunty Shirley Kauhaihao, Ngaire Gilmour, Neil Logan, Sophia Bowart, Ernst Göstch, Henrique Sousa, Randy Thaman, and Angelina and Mike McCoy.

Diane is deeply grateful to the many residents of Pohnpei, Kosrae, Chuuk, and American Samoa who helped her see and begin to understand the agroforests encompassing the breadfruit trees! She owes a tremendous debt to Adelino Lorens and his extended family, Faga Malaga, Madison Nena, and Sleeper Sared. This work is an homage to Bill Raynor, an incomparable agroforester and conservationist in Pohnpei who joined her on this breadfruit journey for 30 years before his untimely passing in 2015.

The regenerative organic breadfruit agroforestry project—of which this handbook is one outcome—was made possible with generous support from Patagonia Provisions® and the State of Hawaii Department of Agriculture. We also received support for this project from Kauai County Office of Economic Development. This publication was also funded by the National Institute of Food and Agriculture, U.S. Department of Agriculture, under award number 2016-38640-25383 through the Western Sustainable Agriculture Research and Education program under subaward number EW17-004 (USDA is an equal opportunity employer and service provider).

AUTHOR BIOS

Craig Elevitch has been an educator in agroforestry since 1993. Craig's internationally recognized publications and workshops have guided thousands in becoming more proficient in ecological food production, agroforestry, and reforestation. In addition to working directly with dozens of farmers, he has facilitated numerous agroforestry workshops in the Pacific, with over 7,000 producers and resource professionals participating since 1993. His agroforestry publications have garnered millions of downloads. These include *Agroforestry Guides for Pacific Islands* (2000), *Traditional Trees of Pacific Islands* (2006), *Specialty Crops for Pacific Islands* (2011), and *Agroforestry Landscapes for Pacific Islands* (2015), all of which promote diverse agricultural systems that are environmentally and ecologically regenerative. He is also co-director of Hoʻoulu ka ʻUlu—Revitalizing Breadfruit and agroforestry director of the Pacific Regional Breadfruit Initiative, projects founded in 2010 to restore breadfruit agroforests in Pacific Island landscapes.

Dr. Diane Ragone is Director of the National Tropical Botanical Garden's Breadfruit Institute, created in 2003 to promote the conservation, study, and use of breadfruit for food and reforestation. She is an authority on the conservation and use of breadfruit. Her horticultural and ethnobotanical studies on this important Pacific staple crop for 35 years resulted in the establishment of the world's largest breadfruit conservation repository with 150 cultivars. She is Affiliate Graduate Faculty at the University of Hawaii in Tropical Plant & Soil Sciences and Ecology, Evolution, & Conservation Biology, and received a MS and PhD in Horticulture from UH. She is co-director of the Hoʻoulu ka ʻUlu project to revitalize ʻulu in Hawaii. Dr. Ragone is author of over 100 publications on breadfruit, horticulture, and native Hawaiian plants. In 2015 she was honored as UH's College of Tropical Agriculture's Distinguished Alumna and in 2016 received the Garden Club of America's Medal of Honor.

PREFACE

Breadfruit, a tree native to the Pacific Islands, is an icon of nature's abundance and the connectivity of Pacific Island culture to the natural world. Breadfruit was traditionally grown in very diverse, multistory forest gardens ("agroforests"), as a means of production that has sustained islanders for thousands of years.

In 1793, British botanist Archibald Menzies wrote of the traditional agroforests of Kona, Hawaii, "… their fields in general are productive of good crops that far exceed in point of perfection the produce of any civilized country within the tropics." Productive agroforests such as those of pre-Western-contact Kona were cultivated throughout the Pacific Islands, and some still exist to various degrees. The gift of breadfruit was disseminated beyond the Pacific to the tropical world over the past 230 years, with peoples in tropical regions of the Caribbean, America, Africa, and Asia adopting it into their landscapes and diets.

In many breadfruit-growing regions, large-scale plantation crops such as sugarcane, coconut, coffee, and root staples replaced breadfruit agroforests. Simultaneously, the trend in agriculture over the past 200 years has been towards simplification in single-commodity plantings or "monocultures." Commercial plantation monocultures came to dominate much of the agricultural landscape, replacing the diverse agroforestry systems in which breadfruit grew together with numerous other crops. In areas of the Pacific heavily impacted by plantations, for example, nearly all of the breadfruit agroforests were removed to make way for plantation crops. In Hawaii, only a small percentage of the original breadfruit trees have progeny that have survived to this day. Additionally, many breadfruit cultivars are threatened in their place of origin due to neglect or environmental changes.

In locations where the agroforests disappeared in the Pacific, so did the agroforestry knowledge. Monoculture agriculture was widely adopted, and diverse agroforestry systems became a distant memory. In fact, not only was the knowledge lost, but the potential for agroforestry as a time-tested, sustainable, regenerative method of producing food was almost forgotten, except by indigenous peoples whose ancestral memory of agroforestry was kept alive.

In recent years, breadfruit has received renewed attention, largely thanks to the dedicated work of many organizations working for food security, local agricultural economy, and environmental restoration. Agroforestry has also received increasing attention for addressing a wide range of pressing environmental, economic, and social issues around the world. Rather than plant breadfruit in monoculture plantations, an agricultural system that prioritizes only commercial production, there is wide interest today in planting breadfruit together with a range of other crops and plants in regenerative systems that meet multiple needs beyond commercial production: local food and nutritional security, conservation and improvement of soils and water quality, and economic/environmental risk reduction.

Clarke and Thaman suggest in their seminal 1993 work *Agroforestry in the Pacific Islands: Systems for sustainability*, "… the gradual disappearance of time-tested agroforestry systems and their component species and varieties … will only be reversed by deliberate planning and action." The purpose of this guide is to point the way for cultivation of breadfruit in agroforestry systems designed for today's socioeconomic and environmental conditions. The ancient multistory agroforestry systems of the Pacific and other tropical regions are a promising initial model for what is possible in terms of long-term productivity using minimal imported inputs. Additionally, there is a wide range of modern techniques to draw upon in developing agroforestry systems that can expand upon indigenous models to further address issues of ecological, economical, and social sustainability in the modern context. Such methods harmonize with organic approaches to food production that simultaneously enhance soil fertility and health, water quality, biodiversity, ecosystem health, and carbon sequestration—regenerative organic agriculture.

By synthesizing the traditional and the modern, this work is intended to contribute in a small way to a new agricultural era in which breadfruit is cultivated for the benefit of human, environmental, and economic health.

Craig Elevitch, Holualoa, Hawaii
Diane Ragone, Kalaheo, Kauai
March 15, 2018

BREADFRUIT AGROFORESTRY
GUIDE

PLANNING AND IMPLEMENTATION OF REGENERATIVE ORGANIC METHODS

By Craig R. Elevitch and Diane Ragone

1 INTRODUCTION

This guide focuses on planning, establishment, and management of breadfruit grown as a major component of multistory agroforestry. It comes at a time of increasing interest in breadfruit, together with worldwide movements toward healthful, locally grown food and regeneration of productive ecosystems. Breadfruit has played an important role in meeting these objectives in traditional Pacific Island agriculture for millennia (Figure 1.1), and will continue to do so if grown in holistically planned and maintained agroforestry systems. Additionally, for the first time in history, breadfruit is being commercialized on a large scale in many tropical locations.[1] This guide suggests ways forward using agroforestry techniques that can support vibrant local food economies while also supporting export markets, where desirable.

The intended audience for this material is commercial producers, agricultural professionals, extension agents, and regional planners, in other words, those who have some agricultural experience and knowledge. Although the concepts presented here carry over well to other environments, the presentation focuses on species and environments where breadfruit grows well, the humid subtropics and tropics.

The material herein is intended for both those who already have experience with agroforestry as well as those who are only familiar with monoculture (single crop) orchards, and those who would like practical guidance for establishing a breadfruit agroforest. The techniques covered are applicable to multistory plantings, that is, plantings that integrate species in the low, medium, high, and overstory levels similar to a natural forest. Multistory agroforestry can be used in production orchards, for boundary plantings such as windbreaks or coastal buffers, and in community and home gardens.

Although economic yields of breadfruit agroforestry are highlighted, there are many other potential benefits beyond the economic ones. This guide is for those who are also looking for practical means to diversify their breadfruit plantings for environmental and social benefits. These are harder to quantify than economic outcomes, but are equally, if not more, impor-

tant, as they address some of the biggest challenges of our time: land degradation, food security, weather extremes associated with climate change, and social disparities. This also guide focuses on regenerative techniques that meet or exceed organic certification standards. Meeting such standards can give producers certain advantages in the marketplace and is consistent with the principles behind multistory agroforestry.

This guide introduces tools for implementing agroforests where breadfruit is a major component, beginning with a general introduction to agroforestry in its historical and modern contexts and an introduction to breadfruit's environmental preferences and culti-

Figure 1.1 Traditional breadfruit agroforests throughout the Pacific Islands have multiple canopy layers and many crops in common. These two multistory agroforests in Hawaii (top) and Samoa (bottom) include many commercial and subsistence crops and can serve as models for regenerative cultivation of breadfruit in a modern context.

1 NWC 2005, Ragone 2011, Roberts-Nkrumah and Duncan 2016

var characteristics. It then guides the reader in planning a multistory breadfruit agroforest. The next section covers establishment, followed by management techniques. The range of value-added products is presented as a backdrop for growing a suite of crops together that complement one another in product development. A big question for commercial growers is how agroforestry compares economically with monoculture production. To address this complex question, a section of commercial considerations and economic analysis for breadfruit agroforestry is included.

As a holistic production system, agroforestry touches on many topics. However, where the material is covered elsewhere, such as harvesting techniques and postharvest processing, we refer the reader to those sources.

1.1 What is agroforestry?

Agroforestry refers to dynamic, ecologically based farming systems that integrate trees, shrubs, and other perennial plants with crops and/or animals in ways that provide economic, environmental, and social benefits.[2] Based on creating an agroecological succession (i.e., applied agroecology[3]), the benefits can be realized in many ways simultaneously, including greater and more diverse productivity, reduction of economic and environmental risks, soil improvements, subsistence and cultural functions, and long-term forest for future generations. One can think of agroforestry as a holistic agricultural management system using the synergistic principles at work in natural forests.

1.1.1 Traditional agroforestry systems

Even though the word agroforestry is relatively new in the English language, the concepts behind it are ancient. In the tropical world, agroforestry landscapes have traditionally been the primary form of production in many regions. Agroforests cultivated around homes—agroforestry homegardens—are considered to be some of the most productive and sustainable agricultural systems in the world. In such agroforestry homegardens, a wide diversity of food-producing trees, shrubs, and seasonal crops are cultivated in carefully maintained relationship to each other. Medicinal, culturally significant, herb, spice, and ornamental

plants are also cultivated in rich diversity because of the close proximity of such gardens to people. It is not unusual to find 100 or more species growing together in such homegardens,[4] a comparable level of biological diversity to that occurring in natural forests. In many regions of the Pacific and elsewhere, it is commonplace to see one or two breadfruit trees growing in every home landscape together with numerous other traditional food, medicinal, and ornamental plants (Figure 1.2).

The traditional systems of the Pacific had the following characteristics that differentiate them from today's conventional agricultural practices[5]:

- Did not depend on external energy or nutrients— i.e., no imported fuel, fertilizers, or other imported materials were required

- Did not receive applications of poisonous chemicals or other pollutants

- Had strongly positive net energy yields—for every unit of energy invested, 18–20 units of food energy were returned

- Used only renewable resources as inputs, rather than imported, often nonrenewable, inputs such as inorganic fertilizers

Figure 1.2 Pacific Island homegardens are models for self-sustaining agriculture that often include breadfruit as an abundant subsistence staple. This Samoan homegarden includes breadfruit and other fruit trees, other staple foods, and ornamentals.

---

2 See Leakey 2017 for additional definitions
3 Altieri 1995, Leakey 1999

4 Kumar and Nair 2007
5 After Clarke and Thaman 1993

- Were structured so that the resources supporting agriculture (energy, land, labor, vegetation) were equitably spread throughout the community rather than being concentrated in the hands of a few or in urban areas
- Contained resources that were preserved for future generations only slightly modified from those that the current generation had inherited
- Were based on diversity of tree and non-tree crops, wild plants, and animals, rather than on monocultures or specialized livestock production.

Through careful observation of natural forests, including how forests reestablish after disturbances such as fires or severe storms, and trial and error over many generations, agroforestry was developed traditionally as a foundation for food production throughout the tropics. In the Pacific Islands, agroforestry systems have been in existence for millennia—up to 9,000 years in Papua New Guinea and 3,000 years in much of Polynesia and Micronesia. These managed systems consisted of primarily multistory food forests that resemble native forests in structure and biological diversity.

1.2 Traditional breadfruit agroforestry

Breadfruit is a signature tree of traditional agroforestry systems throughout Oceania on volcanic islands as well as low-lying coral atolls. The landscape coverage, complexity and diversity of plants (Table 1.1) grown with breadfruit varies from island to island depending upon geology, environmental conditions, and local preferences. Breadfruit, along with coconut palms, native trees, and introduced timber species form the high canopy in these agroforests. Breadfruit agroforests on the island of Pohnpei, Federated States of Micronesia, epitomize these systems by incorporating more than 120 useful species, including 50 cultivars of breadfruit.[6] In Micronesia, breadfruit is frequently used as a trellis tree for yam (*Dioscorea* sp.) cultivation.

Over the past 300 years, hundreds of new crops and other plant species have been brought to the Pacific Islands through continued waves of migration from other regions. Many of these introduced crops have been adopted into local diets and incorporated into agroforestry plantings, becoming "traditional" crops of the local people. Similarly, as breadfruit and other plant species were introduced to the Caribbean Islands and West Africa, smallholder farmers planted breadfruit trees with other useful and desired plants. Animals, especially chickens, pigs, and goats, are also integral elements of these traditional breadfruit agroforests.

Grown in a small area near the home, agroforestry homegardens are a microcosm of landscape-scale agroforests, with breadfruit, other fruit trees, vegetables, root crops, herbs, ornamentals, medicinal plants, including all plants the family needs and wants. This type of home food forest has organically developed in

Table 1.1 Crops that are often grown together with breadfruit in traditional Pacific Island agroforestry (after Elevitch et al. 2015).

Years crop is present	Low (up to 2 m [6.5 ft])	Medium (2–5 m [6.5–16 ft])	Tall (5–8 m [16–26 ft]) and Overstory (8+ m [26+ ft])
Years 1–3	annual vegetables pineapple (*Ananas comosus*) taro (*Colocasia esculenta*) pumpkin and squash (*Cucurbita* spp.) sweet potato (*Ipomoea batatas*)	giant taro (*Alocasia macrorrhiza*) papaya (*Carica papaya*) sugarcane (*Saccharum officinarum*)	
Many decades beginning in Year 1	ti (*Cordyline fruticosa*)	banana (*Musa* spp.) cacao (*Theobroma cacao*) coffee (*Coffea arabica*) kava (*Piper methysticum*) noni (*Morinda citrifolia*)	betel nut (*Areca catechu*) citrus (*Citrus* spp.) coconut (*Cocos nucifera*) poumuli (*Flueggea flexuosa*) sago palm (*Metroxylon* spp.) Tahitian chestnut (*Inocarpus fagifer*) yam (*Dioscorea* spp.) Various timber trees

6 Fownes and Raynor 1993, Ragone and Raynor 2009

most areas where breadfruit is cultivated. Only over the past 10–20 years have breadfruit trees been planted in single-crop orchards.

1.3 Modern agroforestry systems

In modern times, a number of agroforestry systems, more commonly known as agroforestry practices, have been developed with various structural characteristics that differentiate them from traditional multistory subsistence agroforestry.[7] Many of these configurations specifically address resource conservation concerns such as wind and water erosion and soil degradation. For example, trees and shrubs can be planted in various configurations to serve as a windbreak. Other configurations can be used to control erosion along waterways and coastlines (buffer zones). In practice, elements from multiple types of systems may be combined to customize an agroforest to suit site characteristics, production goals, and human preferences.[8]

This guide focuses on multistory agroforestry, which we define as diverse plantings of trees, shrubs, vines, and herbaceous plants occupying three or more canopy layers continuously throughout the agroforest's life (Figure 1.3). Although we focus here on commercial orchard configurations, multistory agroforestry can be used in windbreaks, boundary plantings, and other configurations, including for subsistence purposes. A list of important agroforestry practices is given in Table 1.2. Even livestock or poultry can be systematically integrated into multistory agroforestry on a permanent or intermittent basis, although such systems are not covered here.

1.4 Why not use conventional single-commodity cropping for breadfruit?

For the past 150 years, the trend in commercial agriculture has been to grow crops in single crop plantings or "monocultures." Tropical crops such as sugarcane, taro, coffee, and banana have all been grown in monocultures worldwide for many decades, and in some cases for over a century. Since the 1940s, which brought widespread use of herbicides, monocultures often are maintained in the absence of any ground cover (aka "clear culture").

Monoculture simplifies planting, management, harvesting, and marketing activities, as a production method that seeks to maximize yields, and thus profits, from a single crop. However, there are a number of serious environmental, social and economic trade-offs, especially for traditional growers, including increased dependency on fossil-fuel-based inputs, susceptibility to pests and disease (see Table 1.3), soil degradation, toxic chemical residues, and loss of the benefits of biodiversity.[9] Also, the world's industrial food production and distribution systems, primarily based on large-scale monocultures that are heavily dependent upon fossil-fuel-based inputs and practices, are estimated to be the source of 14–18% of greenhouse gases released due to human activity.[10]

Farm enterprises that practice monoculture are also vulnerable to fluctuating market demand and prices. During a severe price downturn of a monoculture crop, large areas can be abandoned, as has occurred with sugarcane, pineapple, and numerous other crops in the Pacific and elsewhere.

Table 1.2 Various agroforestry practices that can have multistory configurations suitable for breadfruit (Torquebiau 2000, Elevitch et al. 2015).

Practice name	Brief description
Buffer zones	Trees and shrubs along waterways, coastline, or other geographic feature
Forest farming	Cultivation of crops under a forest canopy
Homegarden agroforestry	Very diverse and usually intricate configurations planted and maintained by household members
Multistory agroforestry	Diverse plantings of trees, shrubs, vines, and herbaceous plants occupying three or more canopy layers
Orchard interplanting	Orchard trees and shrubs grown together with annual or perennial crops
Windbreak/ shelterbelt	Trees and shrubs planted as a permeable barrier to redirect, filter, and slow wind.

7 see NAC (www.fs.usda.gov/nac/practices/), ICRAF (www. worldagroforestry.org), and Elevitch et al. 2015
8 Elevitch 2015

9 Altieri 2007
10 Pachauri et al. 2014

Figure 1.3 This guide focuses on multistory agroforestry (agricultural land use practice) where breadfruit (the crop of interest) is a major component. In this young Samoan agroforest, crops include noni, cacao, poumuli, and coconut in addition to breadfruit.

1.5 Why agroforestry?

1.5.1 Economic benefits

There are many ways that producers can benefit from agroforestry. The productivity of any one crop in agroforestry may be less than a monoculture of that crop on the same area, however, the total productiv-

ity (combined yield of all the crops growing together) can exceed that of monocultures by 10–60%.[11] In other words, instead of maximizing production of a single crop, agroforestry optimizes the production of the whole system (total productivity), which often exceeds that of any one of the crops grown by itself. As with all crops, producers enter the market when they see a profitable opportunity, increasing the supply and depressing prices. Excess production can then lead to market gluts and low prices, therefore, having a diverse crop portfolio can be a big advantage that provides multiple sources of revenue. As long as crop prices are independent of one another, a diverse set of crops is less impacted by fluctuations in market prices.

Another advantage of agroforestry is the opportunity to cultivate short-term crops in the space between long-term crops, leading to income streams long before the breadfruit trees are bearing commercial quantities (Figures 1.4–1.5). Early income streams can significantly offset costs beginning in the first year. For family-operated farms, having multiple crops opens opportunities to more evenly distribute farm labor demands throughout the year, reducing the need to hire

Table 1.3 A comparison of severe epidemics in native crops of the Pacific Islands suggests potential for breadfruit to also be susceptible to pest and disease problems exacerbated by monoculture cultivation (Nelson 2006).

Crops & diseases (pathogen)	Development of severe epidemics	
	In monoculture	In agroforestry
Kava		
Kava dieback (CMV)	Yes	No
Shot hole (*Phoma*)	Yes	No
Root knot (*Meloidogyne*)	Yes	No
Noni		
Black flag (*Phytophthora*)	Yes	No
Root knot (*Meloidogyne*)	Yes	No
Banana		
Panama wilt (*Fusarium*)	Yes	No
Sigatoka (*Mycosphaerella*)	Yes	No
Bunchy top (BBTV)	Yes	No

Figure 1.4 Coffee growing together with macadamia nut (*Macadamia integrifolia*), a simple agroforestry configuration, has been adopted by many farmers in Hawaii. The coffee produces commercial quantities several years before macadamia nut, helping with early cash flow. The crops grow well together when the macadamia nut is pruned. Their maintenance and harvest schedules spread labor demands more evenly throughout the year than only either one of the crops.

11 Mead and Willey 1980

outside labor. Also for family farms, having multiple crops can contribute to a healthier and well-balanced family diet, reducing the need to purchase food. Because of annual peak seasons in production, breadfruit lends itself well to local as well as export markets (Figure 1.6).

1.5.2 Environmental benefits

In addition to higher total productivity, agroforestry systems can provide a wide range of environmental services that address soil and water resource concerns through erosion control, improvement of soil health, and wind shelter. Diverse agroforestry systems are generally more resistant to pests and diseases than monocultures[12] and benefit biodiversity/wildlife.[13]

As the global climate changes, we can expect to encounter more frequent weather extremes of drought, more intense rainfall events, and tropical hurricanes/cyclones and associated flooding. Agroforestry has been shown to be resilient to weather extremes (Figure 1.7), as stated in recent climate change reports,[14] "Acknowledging the importance of soil health and fertility, diversity, and climate-resilient agroforestry systems has to be the overriding adaptation response in agriculture to climate change." In particular, because of breadfruit's tolerance of climate variability and compatibility with other crops in agroforestry, it is seen as an ideal crop for future production systems.[15]

Other environmental benefits include:

- Crop yields tend to increase over time due to reduced water evaporation and transpiration from plants (evapotranspiration), buffering from drastic weather shifts, reducing wind damage, suppressing invasive weeds, and improving soils[16]

- Multistory agroforestry systems create habitat for beneficial species, which may reduce losses from pests and diseases

- Multistory agroforestry has been shown to sequester carbon from the atmosphere more effectively that other land uses.[17]

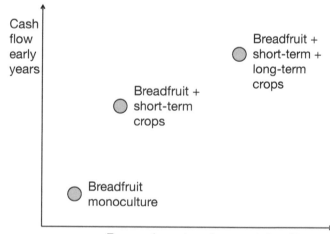

Figure 1.5 Early cash flow vs. economic and environmental resilience for breadfruit monoculture, breadfruit with short-term crops, and breadfruit with short- and long-term crops.

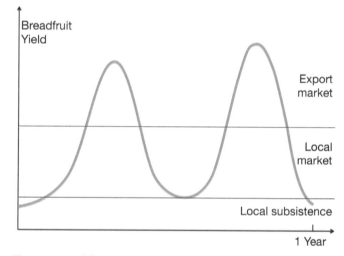

Figure 1.6 The annual cycle of breadfruit yields (thick green curve) with peak seasons lends itself well to providing for subsistence, local markets, and export markets. Instead of going to waste, surpluses during the harvest peaks can be used for value-added products and export.

- A mixture of trees and shrubs creates an extensive root network that captures nutrients from different soil levels before they are carried away by rainfall

- A diverse structure is provided for biodiversity of macro- and micro-organisms.

1.5.3 Social benefits

Multistory agroforestry provides a basis for community self-sufficiency that is resilient to weather extremes by increasing local food and nutrition security (Sec-

12 Pumariño et al. 2015
13 Leakey 2014
14 Bell and Taylor 2015; Thomson and Thaman 2016
15 Tora et al. 2014
16 Wilkinson and Elevitch 2000
17 Toensmeier 2016

tion 2.1) and enhancing preparedness in case of a major interruption of food distribution. By purposefully diversifying local crop production, breadfruit agroforestry opens opportunities for innovation in product development.

The livelihood benefits from income generation and offsetting food expenses can contribute to basic needs such as schooling, health care, nutrition, and local employment. Multistory agroforestry also provides opportunities for agricultural work at various skill levels, from planning, implementation, maintenance, harvest and postharvest, and marketing. Agroforests create a shadier work environment in which temperatures are cooler during the day as compared with open fields and row crop agriculture.

By its nature, multistory agroforestry allows for integrating culturally important plants, connecting the landscape to people and their heritage. One of the most important social benefits for many people is to leave a lasting legacy for future generations, as the trees in an agroforestry system can provide benefits for decades or centuries.

Figure 1.7 Breadfruit bearing a normal size crop in Vanua Levu, Fiji during an extreme drought period in 2014 when annual crops such as taro and sweet potato were failing.

1.6 Disadvantages of agroforestry

Agroforestry combines multiple economic, environmental, and social objectives, and therefore there is no fixed "recipe" or plan for implementation. Each site is different, markets for crops vary, and personal preferences are unique. A focused effort is required for planning, establishment, and management. One

Table 1.4 Comparative advantages and disadvantages of commercial agroforestry and monoculture.

	Agroforestry	Tree crop monoculture
Advantages	Multiple crops, more options, better risk management Early returns Higher total productivity Resistant to pests and diseases Resilient response to weather extremes Provide environmental services (improved soil, carbon sequestration, erosion control, etc.) Crop maintenance rather than weed control	Simpler to plan and manage Laborers require less skill Easier to mechanize Maximizes production of one crop
Disadvantages	No recipe for implementation Knowledge intensive More complex management Timing of management is very important More difficult to mechanize certain operations	Reliance on market for a single crop More susceptible to pests and diseases Not using all ecological niches, so lower total productivity Surges and lulls in labor demand No early yields, all negative early cash flow Clean culture (use of herbicides) results in soil erosion, nutrient losses, and degradation Herbicide can impact breadfruit tree health through uptake by surface roots or root shoots

can expect that all of these activities will be more demanding than for a monoculture. The planning phase requires identifying a suite of crops that not only will grow well together on the site, but that have a commercial market or other desired use (such as home consumption). Management interventions are more complex and time sensitive in agroforestry. Because of the complexity of the overall planting, knowledge and experience are even more important than with monoculture cultivation. Weighing these disadvantages with the advantages of agroforestry is an important part of the planning process for producers, educators, community leaders, and policymakers (Table 1.4).

2 BREADFRUIT CULTIVARS AND BREADNUT

There is extensive diversity of breadfruit (*Artocarpus altilis* [Parkinson] Fosberg) cultivars in the Pacific region, as well as numerous hybrids between breadfruit and its close relative dugdug (*A. mariannensis*) in Micronesia. Hundreds of named cultivars (varieties) have been selected over centuries by farmers and cultivated on volcanic islands and low-lying coral atolls. Some cultivars are widely distributed and grown on many islands and known by different names depending upon the location, such as 'Maopo' in Samoa and Tonga, which is known as 'Mei aukape' in Marquesas, 'Uto lolo' in Fiji, 'Morava' in the Cook Islands, and 'Sra fon' in Kosrae. Others (such as 'Meitehid' in Pohnpei and 'Afara' in French Polynesia) are unique to a certain island or island group. While most people outside of the Pacific region—and even in Hawaii and eastern Polynesian—are only familiar with the Polynesian types of breadfruit that never produce seeds, there are numerous cultivars that contain few to many seeds.[18]

Pacific Islanders preferentially selected and propagated seedless and few-seeded cultivars. Until recently, only a small fraction of Pacific breadfruit diversity has been shared outside of the region. More than 200 years ago, fewer than 10 seedless cultivars were transported from French Polynesia and Tonga by the British and French, respectively, to the Caribbean. These seedless cultivars were then introduced to other countries throughout the Neotropics, Africa,

Breadfruit cultivars (cultivated varieties)
Breadfruit cultivars have a range of characteristics that are important considerations in the agroforestry design and market planning. See Table 2.1 for detailed information on fruit size and quality and tree size and growth habit.

and Asia. Breadfruit is now grown in 90 countries.[19] The few dense-fleshed, starchy seedless cultivars introduced to the Caribbean—generally referred to simply as 'White' or 'Yellow'—subsequently form the base of breadfruit cultivation throughout tropical regions wherever this crop is grown outside the Pacific Islands.

An important tree crop closely related to breadfruit and often mistakenly called "seeded breadfruit," breadnut (chataigne, castaña, *A. camansi* Blanco) is native to Papua New Guinea, and to New Guinea and possibly the Moluccas (also known as the Maluku Islands, Indonesia) and the Philippines. This species was collected in the Philippines by the French in the late 1700s and had a parallel time frame of introduction and distribution to other tropical regions to that of breadfruit.[20] Rather than being grown for its starchy flesh, breadnut contains little pulp and is valued for its numerous protein-rich seeds, which are similar to chestnuts in size, flavor, and texture, and tend to taste sweeter than breadfruit seeds, which can be somewhat astringent. The seeds of both crops are eaten roasted or boiled and cannot be eaten raw. After cooking until tender, the seeds are peeled, salted and seasoned and eaten "out of hand" or mashed to make hummus-like vegetarian spreads or pâté. The culinary uses and potential value-added products using breadnut are largely unexplored at this time. Breadnut can be grown together with breadfruit in agroforestry systems, although the management and marketing of their fruit differ significantly (Figure 2.1).

In the past decade, several different Pacific cultivars conserved in the National Tropical Botanical Garden's breadfruit germplasm repository—produced using micropropagation methods—have become widely available through NTBGs Breadfruit Institute and Global Breadfruit™, and planted in more than 40

---

18 See Ragone 1997 and Zerega et al. 2004 for details on the domestication, diversity, and distribution of breadfruit

19 Ragone and Cavaletto 2006
20 Ragone 1997, 2006; Roberts-Nkrumah 2005; Aurore et al. 2014

countries in Africa, the Caribbean, Central and South America, Asia, and Oceania. These cultivars supplement and complement the common 'White' and 'Yellow' types. Two of these cultivars, 'Ma'afala' and 'Ulu fiti', often contain one or a few seeds (especially 'Ulu fiti'), but are only propagated using vegetative methods. Seeded breadfruit cultivars should not be confused with breadnut.

2.1 Nutritional composition

Breadfruit is an energy-rich food, high in complex carbohydrates, low in fat, and a good source of fiber and minerals such as iron, potassium, and calcium. Some cultivars are good sources of antioxidants and pro-vitamin A carotenoids. All of the essential amino acids are found in breadfruit protein, which is especially rich in phenylalanine, leucine, isoleucine, and valine. It is a nutritionally higher quality protein than occurs in other staple foods such as corn, wheat, rice, soybean, potato, and yellow pea. Cooked breadfruit has a low to moderate glycemic index which could be beneficial in controlling diabetes.[21]

Breadnut seeds are higher in protein than carbohydrate-rich breadfruit and a nice complement to breadfruit nutritionally. Boiled seeds, on a fresh weight basis, contain 4% protein, 10% fiber, and are low in fat (2%) compared to nuts such as peanuts or almonds. The seeds are high in potassium and phosphorus and provide 8 of 10 essential amino acids. The oil is a good source of edible fat and compares well with the unsaturated fatty acid composition of melon seeds, soybean, and peanut. It is rich in oleic and linolenic acids; the latter is an essential fatty acid that must be obtained from food.[22] Flour made from breadnut seeds contains 13–19% protein by dry weight (DW).[23]

2.2 Environmental preferences and tolerances

In general, breadfruit and breadnut are crops for the hot, humid tropical lowlands. The latitudinal optimum is between approximately 17°N and 17°S; but trees are cultivated as far north and south as 23.5° (Figure 2.2). Trees do best at daytime temperatures of 21–32°C (70–90°F), although they can be productive at temperatures as high as 40°C (104°F) and as low as

15°C (59°F), depending upon growing conditions. The tree will grow, but yield and fruit quality will suffer when nighttime temperatures are consistently cooler than 10°C (50°F).[24]

General rainfall requirements are 1500–3000 mm/yr (60–12 in/yr). Rain stimulates vegetative growth, flowering, and rate of growth of the fruit. Annual rainfall of 1500–2500 mm (60–100 in) is considered optimal, although trees will yield regularly in areas that receive more than 1000 mm of rain annually. Breadfruit prefers rainfall of fairly equal distribution throughout the year, but is quite tolerant of short dry periods. For more detailed environmental requirements, see Tables 2.1–2.2.

Figure 2.1 Breadfruit has a dense, leafy canopy (top) that often form an apron down to the ground, while breadnut (bottom) has a relatively open canopy and tends not to have low branches.

21 Jones et al. 2011, 2013; Liu et al. 2015; Turi et al. 2015
22 Williams and Badrie 2005; Adeleke and Abiodun 2010
23 Jones et al. 2011
24 Ragone 1997, 2006

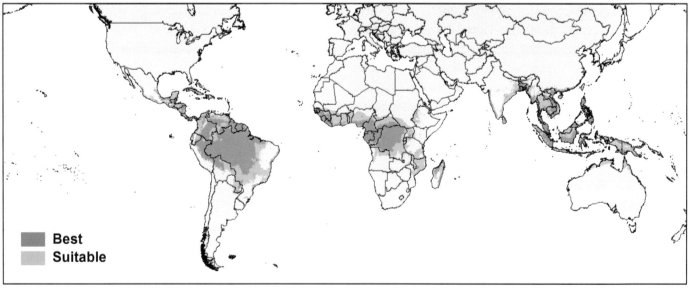

Figure 2.2 Breadfruit suitability map showing zones of "best" and "suitable" growing conditions for breadfruit, modeled from WorldClim data of rainfall and temperature (Lucas and Ragone 2012). A searchable web-based global map of suitable breadfruit growing areas based on rainfall and temperature parameters is available at goo.gl/fCQt41.

Seeded and seedless hybrid breadfruit cultivars (*A. altilis* × *A. mariannensis*) are well adapted to coral atoll environments (e.g., calcareous soils, salt spray, higher saline conditions), while typical seedless Polynesian cultivars tend to not do as well in these environments. 'Maʻafala' has been reported to be tolerant of sandy soils and coastal growing conditions.

Planting breadfruit and breadnut in an agroforest using cover crops and mulches helps to retain soil moisture. Cover crops are a key component to soil regeneration, improving structure, and fertility, carbon sequestration and microbiological diversity. Appropriate drought-tolerant complementary species and windbreaks will help mitigate the challenges of growing these trees in arid environments, and help reduce stress during drought periods.

2.3 Breadfruit productivity

Breadfruit begins bearing in 3–5 years after planting depending upon the cultivar, local environmental conditions, and type and quality of propagation material (see Section 2.5). Trees can produce fruit for many decades. Breadfruit is believed to be one of the most productive crops in the world, with yield estimates under orchard conditions ranging from 16 to 50 metric tons (t) per hectare (ha) (6.5–20.2 t/ac[25]) of fruit (fresh weight [FW]) based on a planting density

> ### Environmental conditions
> Breadfruit grows well in a fairly broad range of conditions. Tables 2.1 and 2.2 show breadfruit's adaptability and ideal conditions. Adaptability varies somewhat with cultivar. Complementary crops grown together with breadfruit should have compatible environmental preferences.

of 100 trees/ha (40 trees/ac).[26] Based on a density of 50 trees/ha, the average projected yield for 4-year-old trees was 1.69 t/ha (0.68 t/ac) FW with yields of 5.23 t/ha (2.12 t/ac) expected after 7 years.[27] Yields of 6.7 t/ha (2.71 t/ac) FW were estimated from land planted with low-input diverse agroforest systems on Pohnpei, Federated States of Micronesia.[28] These yields compare favorably with the average global yields of rice, wheat, or corn at 4.1, 2.6, and 4.0 t/ha (1.7, 1.1, and 1.6 t/ac), respectively.[29]

Annual breadfruit yields per tree vary depending upon cultivar, tree age, condition, canopy height and diameter, and growing conditions, and have been reported to range from less than 100 to more than 900 fruit per tree with average yields of 150–250 fruit, and as high as 400 fruit per tree. The average production for 16 four- to eight-year-old trees was 47–240 fruit per

---

25 Per acre (ac) quantities are given in metric tons (2204 lb), which is similar in weight to a long ton (2240 lb)

26 Ragone 1997, 2006; Jones et al. 2010
27 Liu et al. 2014
28 Fownes and Raynor 1993
29 Jones et al. 2011

Table 2.1 Acceptable and ideal environmental conditions for breadfruit.

Environmental condition	Acceptable range	Ideal range
Elevation range	0–1,500 m (0–5,100 ft), depending on latitude	below 600–650 m (2,000–2,160 ft)
Mean annual rainfall	1,500–3,000 mm (60–120 in), but trees can yield regularly in areas that receive 1,000 mm (40 in).	1,525–2,540 mm (60–100 in)
Rainfall pattern	-	Prefers climates with bimodal rainfall
Dry season (consecutive months with <40 mm [1.6 in] rainfall)	3–6 months (varies depending on cultivar)	No dry season
Mean annual temperature	15–40°C (59–104°F)	21–32°C (70–90°F)
Mean maximum temperature of hottest month	32–38°C (90–100°F)	-
Mean minimum temperature of coldest month	16–18°C (61–64°F)	-
Minimum temperature tolerated	5–10°C (41–50°F). At low temperatures, it may drop leaves and shoots, not yield fruit, and die back.	Above 10°C (50°F)
Soils	Light and medium soils. It requires freely draining soils, neutral to alkaline (pH 6.1–7.4)	Deep, fertile, well-drained soils. Some cultivars are adapted to the shallow sandy soils of coral atolls.

year (48–260 kg or 106–572 lb) in a mixed cultivar orchard in NTBG's McBryde Garden. Some trees produced close to 300 fruit in a year. Trees were pruned to keep their canopy height at 6–7 m (20–23 ft) and diameter at approximately 10 m (33 ft). Breadfruit yield in a multistory agroforestry system on Pohnpei was recorded for 87 trees of five cultivars,[30] with the average number of fruit ranging from 93 to 219 fruit per cultivar with a maximum fruit number ranging from 212 to 615.

Estimates of yield vary widely, and it is difficult to accurately extrapolate yields on a per unit basis from yields of individual trees. For example, managed multiple crop breadfruit groves of Kona, Hawaii Island (traditionally called the *kauulu* zone)—in the centuries prior to European contact in 1778—with 62 trees/ha (25 trees/ac) produced an estimated 1.3–2.6 t/ha (3.1–6.3 t/ac) of fresh fruit. These figures were obtained using an average of 100 fruit per tree and an individual fruit weight of 1.14 kg and 2.28 kg (2.5 lb and 5.0 lb), respectively.[31] Actual fruit counts from 54 5–25+-year-old trees of the Hawaiian 'Ulu' cultivar in this zone in recent times

---

30 Fownes and Raynor 1993
31 Meilleur et al. 2004

Table 2.2 Breadfruit's environmental tolerances.

Drought	Breadfruit can withstand drought for a few months but will prematurely drop its fruits.
Shade	Young trees prefer 20–50% shade but can be grown in full sun.
Fire	It can sprout back from the roots after a small fire, but the trunk and branches are not fire-tolerant.
Frost	It is damaged by frost, which causes it to lose all fruits and leaves, and some branch dieback and even tree death may occur.
Waterlogging	It can tolerate waterlogged soils for only brief periods. Trees have declined and died when standing in water only a few days.
Salt spray	It can tolerate some salt spray for brief periods (same as above), but the leaves will turn yellow and drop off (some cultivars are more tolerant than others).
Wind	The branches break and shed in heavy winds, especially with a heavy fruit load, but shoots and branches quickly regrow.
Special soil tolerances	Depending upon the cultivar, tolerates well-aerated brackish soils, as well as coralline soils and atolls.

had an average yield of 248 kg/yr (546 lb/yr) with yields from individual trees ranging from 159 to 429 kg/yr (350–944 lb/yr).[32]

Factors affecting yield in a traditional agroforestry system are complex and include cultivar differences in phenology (seasonality), growth form, yield, environment (soil moisture and pH, elevation, etc.), disease occurrence and spread, as well as tree canopy size.

2.4 Breadnut productivity

Breadnut is most often grown for its edible seeds—which are removed from the pulp of soft, ripe fruit once it falls from the tree—and there is much variation in seed number, size, and nutritional composition. Large, mature trees have been reported to produce 600–800 fruit per season,[33] but a more realistic figure is 100–200 fruit. The average seed number ranges from 32 to as many as 150 per fruit, each seed weighing an average of 7.7–10 g (0.27–0.35 oz), comprising 30–50% or more of the total fruit weight.[34] Based on tree age and management practices, seed production varies dramatically from year to year, averaging 10–60 kg (22–132 lb) per tree.

Breadnut is fast growing in favorable conditions, growing 0.5–1.5 m (1.5–5 ft) in height per year for the first 10–12 years. The trunk often reaches a height of 3–5 m (10–16 ft) before branching. The tree typically forms large buttresses and extensive spreading surface roots which must be considered when incorporating it into an agroforestry planting. Breadnut tends to have a more open branching structure and sparser canopy than breadfruit. In the Caribbean, heavy pruning was followed by severe and prolonged dieback of the remaining shoots, which significantly limited canopy regrowth and yield compared to breadfruit. Timing and extent of pruning are critical considerations for breadnut as they are for breadfruit.

2.5 Propagation

Breadfruit is typically vegetatively propagated using adventitious root shoots or root cuttings.[35] Trees grown using this method tend to take 3 or more years to begin fruiting. Vegetative propagation is required for seedless cultivars and preferred for seeded cultivars. Seeds of breadfruit are rarely used because seedlings are not true-to-type and can take several years before bearing fruit, although breadnut is always propagated from seed. Young branches and shoots can be air layered (marcotted). Seedless cultivars can be grafted onto seeded rootstock using various techniques such as approach grafting or cleft grafting. Under good conditions, grafted trees can begin bearing in 2 years. Since the mid-2000s, micropropagation techniques have been developed to vegetatively propagate breadfruit in the laboratory using *in vitro* (tissue culture) methods, producing vigorous, disease-free plants (see Section 4.8). Micropropagated trees can begin bearing in 2½–3 years.

2.6 Seasonality

Breadfruit tends to have one large season, often followed a few months later by a smaller, secondary season. However, harvest season varies with cultivar and a cultivar's seasonality can differ from place to place and year to year, even in a limited geographic area such as the Hawaiian Islands. The breadfruit season in most locations begins around the date the sun reaches zenith (the day when the sun passes directly overhead at noon between the Tropics of Cancer and Capricorn) prior to the summer months—a date that varies by latitude—and extends throughout the summer months.[36]

Timing of precipitation and temperature variation may also play a significant role in breadfruit seasonality and their effects need to be studied. For example,

---

Growing several cultivars

Planting different cultivars in an orchard has many advantages, such as an extended period of yield and availability of fruit and different fruit quality, texture, flavor, and nutritional attributes to satisfy different markets, products, and consumer preferences (see Table 2.4). Cultivars may be chosen to complement the expected harvest seasons of the other crops in an agroforest to more evenly spread out labor demands over the year or for making products with multiple ingredients grown together with breadfruit. Grouping the trees by cultivar or season will simplify harvest and handling.

---

32 Lincoln and Lagefoged 2014
33 Parsons 1933 in Coronel 1983
34 Roberts-Nkrumah 2005; Ragone 2006; Liu et al. 2014
35 Ragone 2006, 2008

36 Jones et al. 2010

Table 2.3 Seasonality of breadfruit cultivars over a 10-year period at Kahanu Garden, Hana, Maui, Hawaii (based on Jones et al. 2010).

	Jan	Feb	Mar	Apr	May	Jun	July	Aug	Sep	Oct	Nov	Dec
Cultivars with global distribution												
Maʻafala[†]												
Mei 1[†] (Piipiia)												
Otea[†]												
Puaa[†]												
Ulu fiti[†]												
White												
Yellow												
Breadnut												
Cultivars with local distribution in Hawaii and other Pacific Islands												
Lipet												
Maopo												
Meinpadahk												
Puou												
ʻUlu												

Color key (percentage of years each cultivar had fruit)

0%	<20%	20–39%	40–59%	60–79%	80–100%

[†] Cultivar distributed by Global Breadfruit™

fruit was produced most frequently between August and January, approximately 3–4 months after the main season of male flower production for 130 cultivars at the National Tropical Botanical Garden's (NTBG) breadfruit germplasm repository in Maui, Hawaii.[37] Timing and duration of male flower and fruit production varied from year to year and among cultivars and 10 distinct seasonality groups were identified. The major fruiting season for a subset of cultivars planted in the McBryde Garden, Kauai occurred from July to November (Table 2.3).[38]

Planting cultivars with complementary seasonality patterns could increase yields for farmers and introduction of new cultivars may allow extended or year-round fruit production in areas which currently only have a limited number of cultivars.[39]

2.7 Fruit size

Fruit size is an important variable to consider and the average weight can vary significantly depending upon the age of the tree and the cultivar. A study of more than 90 breadfruit cultivars[40] reported fruit weights from 0.47 kg to 3.54 kg (1.0–7.8 lb), averaging 1.6 kg (3.5 lb). Fruit weighing nearly 5 kg (11 lb) have been harvested from the Micronesian cultivar 'Lipet'.

Producers and consumers, especially in the Caribbean and West Africa, are more familiar with the attributes—size, texture, and flavor—of the commonly grown seedless Polynesian breadfruit cultivars. The edible portion of these cultivars—skin and core removed—averages 83%. Larger fruit obviously provide advantages for processing as they provide larger slices/chunks, but core size can be relatively large (13% vs. 6–7%) in some cultivars of similar size and weight, reducing the edible portion available for use. Depending on the end use, incorporating the skin and/or core with the pulp will increase the amount of fruit available for processing. Consumers with large families and some processors may prefer large fruit in general because they provide more food per unit, but some consumers like smaller fruit for home meals. The smaller size (0.6–1.1 kg or 1.3–2.4 lb) of 'Maʻafala' compared

37 Jones et al. 2010
38 Liu et al. 2014
39 Fownes and Raynor 1993; Redfern 2007; Jones et al. 2010

40 Jones et al. 2011

Table 2.4 Characteristics of breadfruit cultivars

Cultivar	Fruit shape	Fruit weight	Fruit size	Edible portion (% flesh)*	Flesh color, seeds, texture at firm mature stage**	Firmness scale 1–3 (tender to firm)**
Cultivars with global distribution						
Ma'afala[†]	Oval	0.4–1.3 kg, avg. 0.8 kg (0.8–2.9 lb, avg. 1.8 lb)	11–19 × 8–14 cm (4–7 × 3–5 in)	83%	Creamy to pale yellow. Seedless to 1–2 or more seeds. Moderate to tender.	2
Mei 1 (Piipiia)[†]	Oval to Heart-shaped	1–2.1 kg, avg. 1.5 kg (2.3–4.6 lb, avg. 3.2 lb)	13–17 × 14–18 cm (5–7 × 5–7 in)	88%	Pale yellow. Seedless. Tender.	1
Otea[†]	Round to Oval	1.4–2.5 kg, avg. 1.8 kg (3.2–5.5 lb, avg. 4.1 lb)	14–19 × 15–17 cm (6–8 × 6 in)	87%	Creamy to pale yellow flesh. Seedless. Solid, firm.	3
Puaa[†]	Round to Oval	1.0–3.1 kg, avg. 1.7 kg (2.2–6.8 lb, avg. 3.7 lb)	12–22 × 12–17 cm (5–9 × 5–7 in)	88%	Creamy to pale yellow flesh. Seedless. Moderate.	2

* Jones et al. 2011; ** Flesh texture when cooked; † Cultivar distributed by Global Breadfruit™

Table 2.4 Characteristics of breadfruit cultivars (cont.)

Cultivar	Flesh texture at soft, ripe stage	Tree habit/Special growing conditions	Typical fruit and leaves[‡]
Cultivars with global distribution			
Ma'afala[†]	Flavorful, with smooth creamy texture when eaten raw or cooked.	Generally a smaller densely branching tree up to 10 m (33 ft) tall with a spreading canopy. Adapted to atoll, coastal conditions.	
Mei 1 (Piipiia)[†]	Flavorful, with smooth creamy texture when eaten raw or cooked.	Tall, trees reach heights of 15 m (50 ft) or more. More rounded, denser canopy than *A. altilis* cultivars.	
Otea[†]	Intermediate in starchiness and sweetness.	Tall, trees reach heights of 15 m (50 ft) or more.	
Puaa[†]	Intermediate in starchiness and sweetness.	Tall, trees reach heights of 15 m (50 ft) or more.	

[‡] Photos of cultivars conserved in NTBGs germplasm repository

Table 2.4 Characteristics of breadfruit cultivars (cont.)

Cultivar	Fruit shape	Fruit weight	Fruit size	Edible portion (% flesh)*	Flesh color, seeds, texture at firm mature stage**	Firmness scale 1–3 (tender to firm)**
Cultivars with global distribution						
Ulu fiti†	Round	1.1–2.8 kg, avg. 1.8 kg (2.4–6.1 lb, avg. 4 lb)	14–21 × 13–20 cm (6–8 × 5–8 in)	70%	Pale to deep yellow. Usually contains 1–2 or more seeds. Moderate.	2
White	Oval to Round	0.9–1.9 kg, avg. 1.4 kg (2.1–4.2 lb, avg. 3.2 lb)	13–21 × 12–16 cm (5–8 × 5–6 in)	87%	White. Seedless. Solid, dense, firm.	3
Yellow	Oval to Round	0.6–1.3 kg, avg 0.9 kg (1.4–2.8 lb, avg. 2.1 lb)	11–15 × 11–14 cm (4–6 × 4–5 in)	87%	Pale to deep yellow flesh. Seedless. Solid, firm.	2
Breadnut (*A. camansi*)	Oval		14–24 × 10–20 cm (6–10 × 4.8 in)	>50% seeds	White. Numerous seeds. Stringy, generally not eaten.	n/a

* Jones et al. 2011; ** Flesh texture when cooked; † Cultivar distributed by Global Breadfruit™

Table 2.4 Characteristics of breadfruit cultivars (cont.)

Cultivar	Flesh texture at soft, ripe stage	Tree habit/Special growing conditions	Typical fruit and leaves‡
Cultivars with global distribution			
Ulu fiti†	Sweet and flavorful, with smooth creamy texture when eaten raw or cooked.	Tall, trees reach heights of 15 m (50 ft) or more. Produces many root suckers, especially in hillside plantings.	
White	More starchy, not as sweet as other cultivars when ripe.	Tall, trees reach heights of 15 m (50 ft) or more.	
Yellow	Intermediate in starchiness and sweetness.	Tall, trees reach heights of 15 m (50 ft) or more.	
Breadnut (*A. camansi*)	Stringy, sweet, generally not eaten.	Tall, trees reach heights of 15 m (50 ft) or greater. More sparse, open canopy than breadfruit.	

‡ Photos of cultivars conserved in NTBGs germplasm repository

Table 2.4 Characteristics of breadfruit cultivars (cont.)

Cultivar	Fruit shape	Fruit weight	Fruit size	Edible portion (% flesh)*	Flesh color, seeds, texture at firm mature stage**	Firmness scale 1–3 (tender to firm)**
Cultivars with local distribution in Hawaii and other Pacific Islands						
Lipet	Ovoid to Heart-shape	1.5–5.0 kg, avg. 2.8 kg (3.3–11.0 lb, avg. 6.1 lb)	18–28 × 14–21 cm (7–11 × 6–8 in)	88%	Pale to deep yellow. Seedless. Soft.	1
Maopo	Oval to Ovoid	2.0–3.1 kg, avg. 2.5 kg (4.5–6.9 lb, avg. 5.5 lb)	16–22 × 16–18 cm (6–9 × 6–7 in)	89%	Pale white to creamy. Seedless. Firm.	3
Meinpa-dahk	Round to Heart-shaped	0.8–1.3 kg, avg. 1.1 kg (1.8–2.9 lb, avg. 2.4 lb)	12–16 × 12–15 cm (5–6 × 5–6 in)	84%	Pale yellow. Seedless. Tender.	1
Puou	Round	0.7–2.5 kg, avg. 1.8 kg (1.6–5.4 lb, avg. 3.9 lb)	13–22 × 11–19 cm (5–9 × 4–7 in)	74%	Creamy to pale yellow. Often contains 1–2 or more seeds. Moderate.	2
'Ulu	Oval	0.9–1.8 kg, avg. 1.3 kg (2.0–3.9 lb, avg. 2.9 lb)	13–17 × 13–16cm (5–7 × 5–6 in)	88%	White to creamy yellow. Seedless. Solid, firm.	3

* Jones et al. 2011, ** Flesh texture when cooked

Table 2.4 Characteristics of breadfruit cultivars (cont.)

Cultivar	Flesh texture at soft, ripe stage	Tree habit/Special growing conditions	Typical fruit and leaves[‡]
Cultivars with local distribution in Hawaii and other Pacific Islands			
Lipet	Very sweet and flavorful, sweet, smooth creamy texture when eaten raw or cooked	Tall, trees reach heights of 15 m (50 ft) or more. More rounded, denser canopy than *A. altilis* cultivars.	
Maopo	More starchy, not as sweet as other cultivars when ripe.	Tall, trees reach heights of 15 m (50 ft) or more.	
Meinpadahk	Very sweet and flavorful, sweet, smooth creamy texture when eaten raw or cooked	Tall, trees reach heights of 15 m (50 ft) or more. More rounded, denser canopy than *A. altilis* cultivars. Adapted to atoll, coastal conditions.	
Puou	Flavorful, with smooth creamy texture when eaten raw or cooked.	Generally a smaller tree up to 10 m (33 ft) tall with a spreading canopy. Produces many root suckers. Adapted to atoll, coastal conditions.	
'Ulu	More starchy, not as sweet as other cultivars when ripe.	Tall, trees reach heights of 15 m (50 ft) or more.	

[‡] Photos of cultivars conserved in NTBGs germplasm repository

Dwarf breadfruit

There are no true dwarf cultivars of breadfruit. 'Ma'afala' and 'Puou' have a more compact shape than most cultivars, but must be pruned to maintain the size and shape suitable for their location and use. 'Puou' is a common Samoan and Tongan cultivar and currently not available commercially or grown outside of Polynesia and Hawaii. Also, there are no dwarfing rootstocks. Breadfruit is sometimes grafted onto breadnut rootstock, but since breadnut is a fast growing tree with buttresses and large surface roots, grafted trees may express those characteristics. Regular pruning is an excellent way to control tree size for ease of harvest and to maintain tree size in an agroforest or homegarden. Although pruning requires labor, it saves considerable time when harvesting and stimulates vigorous new branch growth, where the fruit is formed.

to more commonly known and grown cultivars such as 'Yellow' and 'White', which average over 1 kg (2.2 lb), is balanced by its excellent nutritional attributes as well as its growth habit.

2.8 Fruit quality

The large diversity of cultivars in the Pacific region allows for variability in fruiting season, productivity, nutritional composition, fruit size, and fruit texture. Flesh texture can be dense, smooth, starchy, creamy, gummy, mealy, fibrous, or stringy, depending primarily upon the structure of the fruit and the species. The fruit is formed from hundreds of tiny flowers attached to a spongy core that fuse together as the fruit develops.[41] The seedless Polynesian types are tightly fused together resulting in a dense, solid texture. In few-seeded cultivars, such as 'Ma'afala', the fusion is not as tight, so the fruit texture is intermediate between the dense seedless types and Micronesian cultivars where the individual flowers are only partly joined, so there is more open space near the core. Moisture content is also a factor. 'Ulu fiti' is only 61% compared to the average 68%,[42] giving this cultivar a firm texture that is different from that of other cultivars now commonly

cultivated and available (similar to a perfectly cooked potato French fry).

The quality of cooked breadfruit at the mature, firm, starchy stage is affected by the method of preparation: different cultivars provide different results when boiled or steamed, roasted, or baked. Some cultivars are suitable for roasting but become soft and fall apart when boiled. In Trinidad, a survey of consumers, food vendors, and processors showed that the 'Yellow' type was preferred over the 'White' type, based on taste. Texture and ease of cooking was not as much of a concern for consumers as for food vendors and processors. In general, 'Yellow' was mainly prepared as a local dish known as "oil down" and by boiling while 'White' was used for frying. This suggests that 'White' cultivars would be more suitable for processing into fries, chips, tostones, and other fried products. Studies of consumer preferences on cultivars and their preparation have not been conducted elsewhere.

The firm flesh of dense starchy cultivars such as the Hawaiian "Ulu', 'Yellow', 'White', and 'Otea' (the latter cultivar available since 2014 through Global Breadfruit™), makes them suitable for many value-added products, such as chips and fries. These and other firm cultivars are more suitable for steaming/boiling for immediate preparation and consumption in an array of dishes or formed into a dough which can then be used. They also lend themselves to freezing and packaging as chunks, fry-cut, or slices for future use.

Softer cultivars, such as 'Ma'afala' and 'Ulu fiti', are more easily mashed after steaming and made into hummus-like and other dips. Their softer texture also makes it very easy to cook and process into a dough which can be used immediately or frozen for future use as a base for baked goods, bread, snack foods, etc. Fruit with seeds are probably unsuitable for large-scale canning, frying, or chip-making operations because seeds interfere with slicing the fruit into the desired shape and size of slices or chunks. Seeded breadfruit can be used in flour making, as the seeds will be ground up and the seed coats sieved out.

Soft, ripe breadfruit can be eaten and used raw in recipes, but is often steamed or blanched at this stage for use as a base for sweet products such as pies or cookies. As with fruit at the firm mature stage, steamed, soft ripe fruit can be frozen for future use. Dense, starchy

---

41 See Ragone 1997 for more details on fruit morphology
42 Jones et al. 2011

cultivars are not as sweet as few-seeded cultivars when fully ripe, making the latter more suitable for use in beverages, desserts, and certain baked goods. There are many Micronesian cultivars, such as 'Meinpadahk' and 'Lipet', that have a softer texture and flavor at both the firm, mature and ripe stages, but their availability is currently limited to islands in Micronesia with a few trees in Hawaii.

In addition to flavor and texture attributes, other considerations for processing include stage of maturity and ease of peeling. Fruit that are too immature (green) will produce profuse milky white sap, making it difficult to peel and cut, with a resulting poor product. Soft ripe fruit would be unsuitable for chips or other products requiring a firm texture. Smooth-skinned cultivars are easier to peel, with less waste.

2.9 Processing/handling/shelf-life

Although breadfruit is edible at any stage of development, it is necessary to understand and recognize the different stages of fruit development and maturity in order to harvest fruit at the optimal stage for the desired market or use (Figure 2.4 and Table 2.5). Fruit picked too green and still immature have a longer shelf life than fruit harvested at the full mature stage, but greener fruit is undesirable for most dishes and products and therefore will disappoint consumers and processors. Determining the optimal stage of maturity to harvest fruit is essential and the grower must rely upon a combination of visual cues such as skin color, scabbing on and around fruit sections, skin texture changes, and less reliably, deposition of dried latex on the surface.[43] Maturity indicators vary by cultivar and in some cases location or even season.

Proper handling will increase shelf life and fruit quality, reduce losses, and help maintain and enhance product value and desirability. The fruit is susceptible to bruising, causing discoloration of the skin and flesh and release of latex, ripening, and decay, when handled improperly. Tall trees are difficult and dangerous to harvest and fruit can easily be damaged by dropping. Never allowing fruit to touch the ground is a key element of food safety best practices. Controlling tree size through regular pruning is an essential component of an efficient and effective harvesting program (see Section 4.6.2).

Breadfruit has a limited fresh shelf life, quickly going from the mature to soft, ripe stage in one to several days once harvested. Proper postharvest handling will help increase shelf life and fruit quality.[44] Freshly harvested fruit fully submerged in cool, clean fresh water can maintain quality for several days or longer. Refrigeration markedly increases shelf life. Satisfactory fruit quality can best be maintained at 12–16°C (54–61°F); at colder temperatures the skin turns an unsightly brown. At these temperatures, a shelf life of 10 days appears possible for untreated fruit and 14 days for fruit wrapped in plastic (Figure 2.3).

Although there exist regional standards,[45] there are currently no nationally or internationally accepted grading standards for breadfruit, with desired size and weight varying by cultivar and market.

Figure 2.3 The shelf-life of fresh, firm mature fruit can be extended to up to 2 weeks by maintaining temperatures of 12–16°C (54–61°F) and wrapping fruits in plastic film. Once the fruit has ripened, it is no longer starchy like potato, but can be used for sweet dishes and desserts.

43 Elevitch et al. 2014

44 See Elevitch et al. 2014
45 e.g., NWC 2005

| Flowering | Immature | Full size green | Mature | Ripe |

| 0 weeks | | ≈16 weeks | ≈20 weeks |

Immature fruit consumed as vegetable. Not preferred for most dishes.

Mature fruit consumed as starch. Preferred for most dishes.

Ripe fruit consumed in sweet dishes

Figure 2.4 Breadfruit can be eaten at all stages of development. However, mature fruit (about 16–20 weeks of development after flowering) has the best eating qualities for most uses (source: Elevitch et al. 2014).

Table 2.5 Generic fruit development for evaluating breadfruit maturity (source: Elevitch et al. 2014).

Development stage	Description/uses	Photo
Flowering (0 weeks)	Breadfruit has both female and male inflorescences. The female inflorescences, commonly called fruit, are edible at any stage of development. Very young fruit have similar taste and texture to artichoke.	
Immature (0–16 weeks)	The deep green fruit at an immature stage of development has a firm, rubbery texture and can be used as a vegetable in dishes.	
Full size green (about 12–16 weeks*)	This is an immature fruit that has reached full size. Despite its longer shelf life, it is not preferred by most consumers. It can be used as a vegetable, but it has not developed starchy characteristics.	

Table 2.5 Generic fruit development for evaluating breadfruit maturity (cont.)

	Development stage	Description/uses	Photo
	Mature (16–18 weeks*)	Mature fruit has developed into a starchy staple with smooth texture and good flavor. It is preferred for most dishes including stews, soups, curries, fries, etc. Fruit harvested in the first two weeks of the mature phase has a longer shelf life than fruit harvested during the second two weeks of maturity.	
	Mature (18–20 weeks*)	Fruit harvested in the latter stages of maturity has excellent eating qualities, but a shorter shelf life than fruit harvested earlier.	
	Half-ripe	After maturity the fruit eventually turns from a starchy staple into a ripe dessert fruit. Half-ripe fruit has begun converting starches into sugars and has a similar texture and sweetness to sweet potato—still slightly firm and moderately sweet. It can be eaten cooked like sweet potato and used in a variety of dishes.	
	Ripe	The fruit eventually turns into a ripe dessert fruit. At this stage the fruit is very soft and emits a sweet, fruity fragrance. Ripe fruit can be used raw (similar to a custard) or cooked in many types of desserts including cakes, cookies, pies, etc.	

* This range is based on a single study of fruit of a typical triploid Polynesian cultivar similar to the Hawaiian 'Ulu'. Data have yet to be collected for 'Ma'afala', 'Ulu', Micronesian hybrid, and other cultivars. Therefore, this time range should be considered a general guide only.

3 PLANNING

As with starting any new commercial farming venture, establishing any new agroforest is a costly undertaking in terms of labor, materials, land resources, and financial investment. Costs encompass land preparation, planting stock, planting, irrigation (where needed), and also significant—maintenance—both short term and long term. The planning process can help optimize the outcomes achieved, while reducing costs and maximizing income potential. A good design can pay for itself many times over in increased yields and avoided costly mistakes or even project failure.

Planning for agroforestry is even more important than planning a monoculture, because there are multiple crops and auxiliary plants (such as ground covers) that must be integrated. Compatible crop selection, spacing, and maintenance are all planning issues to consider in advance of establishment. A key to success in agroforestry is "the right plant in the right place at the right time." In this sense, agroforestry is a knowledge-based, dynamic production system, which benefits greatly from a thoughtful planning process. Best practices in planning have the following benefits

- Optimize use of available resources (people, land, capital)
- Maximize potential total productivity
- Tailor the agroforest to environmental conditions and markets, reducing risks from weather and economic forces
- Evaluate the advantages and disadvantages of different planting configurations

Planning consists of collecting site and market information, evaluating crop options, and then developing an implementation plan (Figure 3.1). There are no fixed formulas for agroforestry, as such systems of crop cultivation are tailored to the site, markets, and personal preferences.

3.1 Site evaluation

A site evaluation gives a comprehensive evaluation of site characteristics and limitations and is an essential part of the planning process. This assessment reveals important considerations related to species selection, soil and water conservation, placement of roads, pathways, and structures, etc., making it critical for an effective plan. Completing a site evaluation often reveals important planning considerations that would not normally come to mind. An example of a site evaluation is given in Section 4.9.

3.2 Complementary crops

A wide variety of annual and perennial crops can be grown together with breadfruit. In agroforests of the Pacific Islands, traditional crops grown with breadfruit include taro, banana, sugarcane, coconut, and many others. Today, dozens of crops and varieties can be considered. This makes crop selection more exciting, but also challenging.

A menu of some potentially complementary crops is included in Table 3.1. Crop selections should be made based on several criteria including:

- Suitability for site conditions (rainfall, temperature, soils, slope, etc.)
- Area/space available
- Availability and quality of plant materials
- Current and anticipated market demand
- Personal preferences
- Family and community subsistence needs
- Complementarity of crop portfolio (markets, processing, etc.).

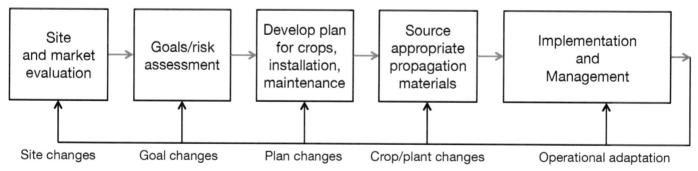

Figure 3.1 Planning is crucial for project success in agroforestry both at the outset and as the project moves forward.

Table 3.1 Short-, medium-, and long-term crops that are compatible with breadfruit and share breadfruit's environmental requirements. These lists serve as a "menu" to select from based on project-specific criteria, including the site conditions, management objectives, markets, and personal preferences.

	Ground (0–1 m)		Low (up to 2 m)
Short term 1–3 yr	ginger (*Zingiber officinale*) poha (*Physalis peruviana*) taro (*Colocasia esculenta*)	turmeric (*Curcuma longa*) vegetables	
Medium term 3–5 yr	pineapple (*Ananas comosus*)		giant taro (*Alocasia macrorrhizos*) kava (*Piper methysticum*) mamaki (*Pipturus albidus*) Pacific spinach (*Abelmoschus manihot*)
Long term 10+ yr	shampoo ginger (*Zingiber zerumbet*)		annatto (*Bixa orellana*) black pepper (*Piper nigrum*) cardamom (*Elettaria* and *Amomum* species) coffee* (*Coffea arabica* and *C. robusta*) gardenia (*Gardenia* species) hibiscus (*Hibiscus* species) ti* (*Cordyline fruticosa*) vanilla (on trellis) (*Vanilla planifolia*)

	Medium (2–5 m)	Tall (5–8 m)	Overstory (8+ m)
Short term 1–3 yr	cassava (*Manihot esculenta*) sugarcane (*Saccharum officinarum*)		yam (seasonal) (*Dioscorea* species)
Medium term 3–5 yr	banana (*Musa* species) papaya (*Carica papaya*) tree tomato (*Solanum betaceum*)	banana (*Musa* species)	
Long term 10+ yr	cacao* (*Theobroma cacao*) citrus* (*Citrus* species) cutnut (*Barringtonia edulis*) longan* (*Dimocarpus longan*) mountain apple (*Syzygium malaccense*) noni* (*Morinda citrifolia*) peach palm (for heart) (*Bactris gasipaes*) puakenikeni (*Fagraea berteroana*) rambutan* (*Nephelium lappaceum*) rollinia* (*Rollinia deliciosa*) soursop (*Annona muricata*) star apple* (*Chrysophyllum cainito*) starfruit* (*Averrhoa carambola*)	avocado* (*Persea americana*) breadfruit* (*Artocarpus altilis*) breadnut* (*Artocarpus camansi*) dugdug* (*Artocarpus mariannensis*) ice cream bean* (*Inga* species) kou* (*Cordia subcordata*) kukui* (*Aleurites moluccana*) lychee* (*Litchi chinensis*) moringa* (*Moringa oleifera*) macadamia nut* (*Macadamia integrifolia*) mango (*Mangifera indica*) mangosteen* (*Garcinia mangostana*) pandanus (*Pandanus* species) sandalwood (*Santalum* species) tamarind* (*Tamarindus indicus*) vi* (*Spondias dulcis*) ylang ylang* (*Cananga odorata*)	betel nut (*Areca catechu*) coconut (*Cocos nucifera*) durian* (*Durio zibethinus*) kamani (*Calophyllum inophyllum*) peach palm (for fruit) (*Bactris gasipaes*) pili nut (*Canarium* species) poumuli (*Flueggea flexuosa*) sago palm (*Metroxylon* spp.) various timber species

* Usually pruned in commercial production and placed in a height category based on pruned height and light requirements relative to other crops.

Moreover, combinations of crops should be selected to fill both horizontal and vertical space in the planting rows throughout the life of the planting.

3.2.1 Cover crops and ground covers

Cover crops and ground covers are used to suppress weeds, prevent soil erosion due to wind and water, to build soil quality, and enhance beneficial soil microorganisms (Table 3.2).[46] "Cover crop" usually refers to temporary, quick cover immediately after soil disturbance or after a cropping cycle is over. Cover crops are especially useful after site preparation for establishing a new agroforest by providing a pulse of organic material and wind protection for the young new crops.

Plants specifically planted as a permanent low cover—but that are not crop plants—are called "ground covers" (as compared with cover crops, which are usually temporary). Ground covers can be used to fill the space between crop plants within crop rows, eliminating space for weeds to germinate and emerge. Additionally, ground covers provide a layer of organic mulch that inhibits erosion and enhances soil properties. Their purpose is to keep the soil covered even during periods when crop plants do not fill the space and where surface mulch has decomposed. Ground covers are selected for shade tolerance and low growth that does not interfere with the crops or create a main-

tenance burden. They should also be inexpensive and easy to propagate.

Unfortunately, there are no perfect ground covers for several reasons. First, each site has unique environmental conditions, favoring some ground cover candidates and hindering others. Second, as conditions change over time (soil, shade, plant interactions), ground covers that once thrived may weaken and be overtaken by other plants. Third, ground covers that grow well may require maintenance to keep them from overtaking crops by climbing. A number of possible ground cover

Table 3.2 Example cover crops and ground covers. Selections should be made based on site conditions and what is locally available (after SOAP 2018).

Cover crops (temporary)	notes
buckwheat (*Fagopyrum esculentum*)	Quick cover, reaches 50 cm, lasts 4–6 weeks
oats (black, *Avena strigosa*, common, *A. sativa*)	Quick cover, reaches 1 m, lasts 8–10 weeks
pigeon pea (*Cajanus cajan*)	Long term cover, 2–4 m, can be cut periodically, lasts 2–3 years
sorghum-Sudan grass hybrids *Sorghum bicolor* x *S. bicolor* var. *sudanense*	Medium term cover, 1–2 m, can be cut periodically, lasts 2–3 years
sunflower (*Helianthus annuus*)	Short-term cover, 1–3 m, lasts 3 months
Sunn hemp (*Crotalaria juncea*)	Short-term cover, 1–1.5 m, can be cut once or twice, lasts 3–4 months
Ground covers (permanent)	notes
beach pea (*Vigna marina*)	Good cover, but climbs other plants, so requires maintenance
comfrey (*Symphytum* spp.)	Forms an effective barrier to many running grasses
hetero (*Desmodium heterophyllum*)	Slow growing, compact ground cover
mucuna bean (*Mucuna pruriens*)	Good cover, but climbs other plants, so requires maintenance
perennial peanut (*Arachis pintoi*)	Moderately tolerant of shade, can form thick thatch, cut periodically
sissoo spinach (*Alternanthera sissoo*)	Edible leaves

46 Evans et al. 1988

plants are listed in Table 3.2. Note that many ground covers used in landscaping are unsuitable to use in the understory of an agroforest, as they demand too much sunlight and care.

3.3 Spacing

Although traditional breadfruit agroforests have provided environmental services and food for millennia, they have several disadvantages that make them unsuitable for today's commercial production methods. These drawbacks include the inefficiencies of activities inherent in "random" or scattered planting configurations with multiple crops and canopy layers. Also, once established, traditional agroforests may receive much less management than is necessary to optimize both the quantity and quality of crops necessary for profitable production. Although well suited for subsistence and resource conservation needs, the addition of commercial production goals suggests significant modern adaptations to the planting configuration used in breadfruit agroforestry as presented in this guide, namely:

- A systematic layout pattern in rows that streamlines management operations, facilitates harvest,

There are no fixed design recipes

The design examples presented here are for illustration purposes only, rather than recipes to follow. Each project is unique and requires thoughtful, customized planning to account for:

- Site conditions (soils, topography, flora and fauna, neighbors, accessibility, etc.)
- Environmental, social, and economic goals
- Available crops and their varieties
- Markets for crops
- Personal experience and preferences
- Local laws, land tenure, community support
- Labor skills and costs

and allows mechanization of certain activities (Figures 3.2–3.3)

- Management techniques such as regular pruning that optimize overall health and productivity of all crops growing together, resulting in high quality products.

This section presents practical application of these two principles.

Common and costly mistakes to avoid

Planting when site conditions are inopportune. Establishment during drought or overly wet periods can lead to disappointing results and defy even the best laid plans. Increasingly, weather patterns seem to be less predictable based on historic averages, meaning that timing for planting is increasingly hard to predict. The onset of the rainy season is usually the best time to begin. **Solution:** The best strategy is to build flexibility into the timing of establishment activities.

Missed maintenance. Lack of timely maintenance can lead to some crops (or weeds) dominating the space and shading out other crops. This problem is often the result of planting too large an area and underestimating the amount of time required for maintenance. Another cause is inattentiveness. **Solution:** Plant an area for which the maintenance can easily be accomplished. Visit the site regularly to evaluate progress and adjust the maintenance schedule.

Poor choice of crops and crop varieties. Sometimes there is a strong temptation to plant crops that are marginally adapted to the site or that do not fit well in the planting configuration. Such temptations often arise from observing successful results in different environments. **Solution:** Select crops that are adapted to similar environments to breadfruit. Establish small trials on-site for any crops that are untested in the region.

Lack of planning. Inadequate preparation can lead to costly mistakes or failure of the project. This is especially true in agroforestry, where complementary crop selection and management timing are crucial for success. **Solution:** Time spent planning the project will pay for itself many times over in avoided losses and maximizing opportunities for additional gains. Consulting with experts and other producers with experience is highly recommended.

Figure 3.2 The scattered planting configuration of traditional agroforests (left) is inefficient for commercial production, especially if machinery or vehicles are to be used. Systematizing operations by organizing crops in rows (right), often planted along curves that follow the land contour, can greatly increase efficiency of management and harvest, which is necessary where cost of production and quality are high priorities.

Conventional monocultures have standard crop spacing and a single crop canopy layer, which makes them relatively simple to design. In agroforestry, one must plan in four dimensions: the three dimensions of space and the time dimension. The three spatial dimensions are the crop spacing on the ground (two dimensions), plus the vertical dimension of canopy layers. The fourth dimension of time refers to the crop composition changing over time as the agroforest matures (whereas the crop is always the same throughout the life of a monoculture).

Figure 3.3 Traditional agroforests are well suited for family and community subsistence consumption, but can often be improved upon for commercial production by systematizing the planting layout for efficient operations.

With horizontal, vertical, and temporal planning all to be determined for a planting, where does one begin making decisions? First, it is best to begin with the assumption that a site has been selected and that it is suitable for cultivation of breadfruit (see Table 2.1). The next step is to choose the cultivars of breadfruit and other complementary crops based on the site conditions, anticipated markets, and personal preferences. Following crop selection, growth rate and management techniques for the crops determine how much space each crop will need over its lifespan. For our purposes, pruning size of the breadfruit is the reference point from which the rest of the crop layout and spacing follows.

3.4 Multistory agroforest

3.4.1 Vertical canopy layers (strata)

By definition, multistory agroforests combine plants that naturally occupy different tree canopy layers. Here, we will consider the agroforest to consist of five layers (Figure 3.4):

• Overstory trees

• Tall trees

• Medium trees

• Low shrubs and small trees

• Ground layer herbaceous plants.

Overstory
Tall
Medium
Low
Ground cover

Figure 3.4 Layers of multistory agroforest. The height of each layer depends upon crop selection and pruning size. Breadfruit occupies the tall layer once it reaches a productive age.

To optimize total productivity, all of these layers are ideally occupied at an appropriate density throughout the life of the agroforest. The heights of these layers are relative to one another. The "model" breadfruit tree used for the purposes of illustration in this guide is shown in Figure 3.5. Others may choose a different pruning size for various reasons, which would affect the whole planting layout.

3.4.2 Succession of crops

When planting a breadfruit agroforest in an open field, there is ample available space between the long-term crop plants. This open space can be dedicated to a range of short-term crops that can generate income while filling ecological niches that nature would like to fill. These early crops complete their life cycles and are phased out as the long-term crops grow, occupying more space above- and below-ground. This natural life cycle process is called succession.

Intercropping means growing two or more crops in close proximity to each other. For example, the space between breadfruit tree rows can be utilized for short-term crops such as turmeric, ginger, taro, and pineapple for a few years. Unless multiple crops are always present in the orchard, it is not considered multistory agroforestry. Section 3.2 covers the time frames and relative heights of complementary crops for a breadfruit agroforestry system.

A wide range of crops can be grown through the succession from open field to a mature breadfruit agroforest. One can see Table 3.1 as a "menu" of crops to select from when planning a succession of crops.

The canopy layer a plant occupies often changes as it matures. As is the case for many trees, breadfruit tolerates more shade when it is young compared with when it is mature. For the first 2–3 years in traditional agroforests, breadfruit occupies the medium layer with up to 50% shade. As the tree grows and matures, it prefers more sunlight until it eventually occupies the tall or overstory layers. Breadfruit grows 0.5–1.5 m (1.5–5 ft) per year, which is slower than many fast-growing crops. For example, young breadfruit trees will develop well in up to 50% shade from short-term crops such as papaya, banana, and tree tomato, crops that will live out their life cycles and be phased out in 3–5 years.

A mature breadfruit tree will grow well with up to 20% shade from open-canopied overstory trees and palms (Figure 3.6). To optimize breadfruit's health and productivity, observation of natural forests suggests moderate shade up to 50% through Year 3 after planting, followed by up to 20% shade for the rest of the breadfruit tree's life. In other words, breadfruit does not necessarily fill the "tall" layer of the emerging agroforest during the first few years, but should occupy the tall layer thereafter.

3.5 Determining space allocated to breadfruit trees

Without pruning, a breadfruit tree often reaches heights of 12–15 m (40–50 ft) or taller with a single trunk and spreading canopy. Such tall trees are inefficient and unsafe to harvest, and unsuitable for commercial production.[47] Every year people around the world are killed climbing tall breadfruit trees.

Spacing is determined by a number of factors, including the pruned size of the trees and desired number of breadfruit trees and other crops in the mature orchard. Each breadfruit tree also requires ample space around it for air circulation to help prevent fruit-borne diseases. Monoculture spacing has been recommended at 8 m × 8–10 m (26 ft × 26–33 ft) for breadfruit pruned to a 6 m (20 ft) canopy diameter.[48] Spacing of 12 m × 12 m (40 ft × 40 ft) with a broader canopy width has also been recommended.[49] The planting configuration in Example 1 (Section 3.7) illustrates spacing with the nominal breadfruit canopy

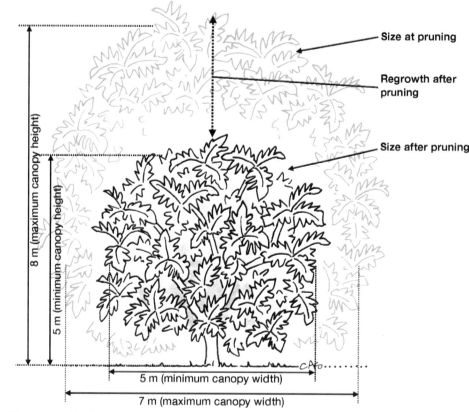

Figure 3.5 Reference sizes before and after pruning of production breadfruit trees used for spacing calculations and layout diagrams used in this guide. Breadfruit trees can be managed at different sizes, depending on harvest operations, site conditions, cultivar, and other crops used, which will affect spacing and layout in the agroforestry design.

width maintained at 5–7 m (16–23 ft). Different spacings would allow for different crop combinations.

Pruning invigorates new growth, which is where new fruit is formed. If pruning begins at an early age, and carried out regularly, breadfruit trees can be kept at a desired size for many decades.[50] For efficient harvest, trees should be pruned to a certain canopy height and diameter that facilitates harvest operations. Pruning size can vary widely depending upon factors such as desired harvest height and the size of neighboring crops. Smaller tree size makes harvesting easier, but reduces the total fruit production per tree. For hurricane prone regions, smaller tree size renders trees less susceptible to breakage of large branches and wind throw (falling over in wind).

3.5.1 Reference space allocation for breadfruit

Individual farmers should choose a pruning size that suits their management style, harvest methods, and other preferences. Since breadfruit can be a major

Figure 3.6 Breadfruit can produce well in light shade, in this case from sparsely planted coconut palms in a traditional agroforest of Samoa.

47 NWC 2005
48 Roberts-Nkrumah 2015
49 Ragone 2006; NWC 2005

50 Elevitch et al. 2014

component in the orchard, planning for crop spacing begins with setting the desired pruned size of the breadfruit trees as a reference for the layout. For the purposes of planning in this guide, a reference pruning height of 5 m (16.5 ft) and canopy diameter of 5 m (16.5 ft) is used. Assuming pruning every 12–18 months to this reference height, trees are expected to grow to a maximum height of about 8 m (26 ft) and canopy diameter of 7 m (23 ft) before the next pruning (see Figure 3.5). These dimensions will be used for reference in spacing diagrams in this guide. If different pruning dimensions are selected, spacing within the planting will need to be adjusted compared to what is presented here.

3.5.2 Space allocated to other crops

For the purposes of planning, Table 3.3 gives example dimensions for canopy height and diameters based on a reference size for breadfruit (shown in Figure 3.5). The actual size crops achieve in the field varies depending upon many factors (cultivars chosen, environment, management, etc.). Many tree and shrub crops are pruned to optimize production and facilitate harvesting, so their size should be managed according to the space needed and available. Spacing for plants that have reached the productive stage should be based upon their pruned size. Until plants reach full size, the space around them can be occupied by vegetation either for crop or organic matter production. Anticipating a productive sequence of crops that fill the available space is one of the biggest challenges of the design process.

Table 3.3 Strata heights and canopy diameters for an example mature breadfruit agroforest. The tall strata height is based upon the reference breadfruit tree size in Figure 3.5 (5–8 m or 16–26 ft), with the other heights set relative to breadfruit. For the purposes of planning, canopy diameters are assumed to be the same as the heights.

Canopy layer	Height and canopy diameter
Overstory	8+ m (26+ ft)
Tall	5–8 m (16–26 ft)
Medium	2.5–5 m (8–16 ft)
Low	1–2.5 m (3.3–8 ft)
Ground	0–1 m (0–3.3 ft)

3.6 Implementation planning and scheduling

The timing of implementation activities is crucial. Once the site is cleared and prepared, it must be planted immediately, or nature will take its course and undesirable weeds will rapidly establish. All materials for implementation including plants and seeds should be ready at the time of site preparation. A rough schedule is given in Table 3.4 for a typical project.

3.7 Example 1: Multistory breadfruit agroforest

Thanks to indigenous Pacific Island farmers, models for breadfruit agroforestry still abound throughout the Pacific, despite the shift towards plantation monocultures in many regions over the past 150 years. Because every site is different, this example should be seen as illustrative, rather than a recommendation. The following 8-crop example (see Table 3.5) is based upon crop selections and spacing from traditional Pacific Island agroforestry. The crops have been cultivated for

Table 3.4 Example implementation schedule.

Time relative to planting the site	Activity
24 weeks before planting (recommended)	Planning, site assessment, project design, begin sourcing and assembling appropriate plant materials. Locate sources of seed and vegetative material for direct planting.
8 to 16 weeks before planting	Start nursery stock timed to be field ready at time of site preparation. Identify sources of mineral and organic amendments recommended based on soil tests.
1 week before planting	Pruning of trees and shrubs that will be integrated into the new planting
Planting time (can be multiple days?)	Site preparation at onset of rainy season, planting immediately after site is prepared
0–4 weeks after planting	Intensive maintenance, watering (if needed)
5+ weeks after planting	Regular maintenance, replanting where needed, harvest, additions of organic matter

Table 3.5 Crops used in Example 1 and their characteristics for planning purposes (adapted from Elevitch 2011).

	Propagation material	Crop production life cycle	Size
Banana (short cultivar)	Sword sucker	Begins in 12–18 months, can continue for many years if managed	For this system, select cultivars of about 5 m (16 ft) in height
Breadfruit	Small field-ready tree from tissue culture, root sucker, air layer, etc.	Begins in 3–4 years, with commercial quantities in Year 5 with productive life of 50+ years	Pruned to stay at height of 5–8 m (16–26 ft) and canopy diameter of 5–7 m (16–23 ft)
Cacao	Grafted seedling	Begins in Year 3 and continues for decades	Pruned to 3–4 m (10–13 ft) in height and canopy diameter
Coconut	Seedling (cyclone-resistant dwarf cultivar for drinking nuts)	Begins in Year 6 with productive life of 40–50 years	Can reach 20 m (65 ft) in productive life with canopy diameter of 10–12 m (33–40 ft)
Kava	Rooted stem cutting	Entire plant harvested in 2–4 years	Up to 3 m (10 ft) tall and 2 m (6.5 ft) canopy diameter
Papaya	Seedling or direct sow	Fruiting begins in 12–18 months with 2–3 years of production before removal	Can reach 10 m (33 ft) tall × 2 m (6.5 ft) in width, but is usually removed at about 5–6 m (16–20 ft) tall
Pineapple	Crowns, slips, or suckers	Fruiting begins in 12–18 months with a productive life through Year 4	Plants can reach 1.5 m (5 ft) in height and 1 m (3.3 ft) in diameter
Taro	Setts (20–30 cm [8–12 in] of stem and top of corm)	Harvest of entire plant at 6–12 months, depending upon cultivar	Reaches 1–2 m (3.3–6.5 ft) in height and canopy diameter

generations in the Pacific, although some were adopted after Western European and Asian contact. Figure 3.7 shows how these crops are grown in traditional Pacific agroforests, suggesting the crop combinations and spacing used in this example.

The principles adapted from traditional systems include:

- Short-, medium-, and long-term crops are interplanted simultaneously after site preparation
- Quick coverage of the area with a dense planting of the crops and other desired plants
- The planting has multiple vertical layers at all ages, including from the beginning
- Longer lived crops replace shorter lived crops as they complete their productive life cycles (succession).

Beyond traditional methods, this example's contemporary adaptations for efficient management include:

- Configuration in rows (preferably along the contour)
- Space between rows is mowed mechanically (or by hand, if machinery is not available and on sloping sites) for organic matter production and ease of access
- Regular, systematic crop spacing for ease of management
- Spacing based upon desired pruned dimensions of the crop trees
- Follow modern crop care guidelines, as possible.

Spacing in this example is determined from traditional spacing observed between trees and other crops in indigenous breadfruit agroforestry systems in Pacific Islands combined with modern agronomic recom-

Table 3.6 The canopy layer occupied by a given crop changes relative to the age of the planting. See Figures 3.8–3.11, which illustrate the table below for Example 1.

	Low	Medium	Tall	Overstory
Year 1	Cacao Kava Pineapple	Breadfruit Coconut Taro	Banana Papaya	–
Year 2–4	Cacao Kava Pineapple	Banana Breadfruit	Papaya	Coconut
Year 5+	Cacao	Banana	Breadfruit	Coconut

Figure 3.7 Example 1 uses crops and crop spacing from traditional Pacific Island breadfruit agroforests, as illustrated in these photos. Upper left: Cacao and banana with coconut and sago palms (Samoa). Note density of planting is 1–2 m (3.3–6.5 ft) between plants. Upper right: In this young breadfruit agroforest crops include banana, noni, cacao, poumuli, and coconut (Samoa). Spacing between plants is 1–3 m (3.3–10 ft). Lower right: Kava, giant taro, and banana growing densely under coconut (American Samoa). Lower left: Approximately 6-month-old planting of sweet potato, cassava, banana, kava, and breadfruit (Hawaii).

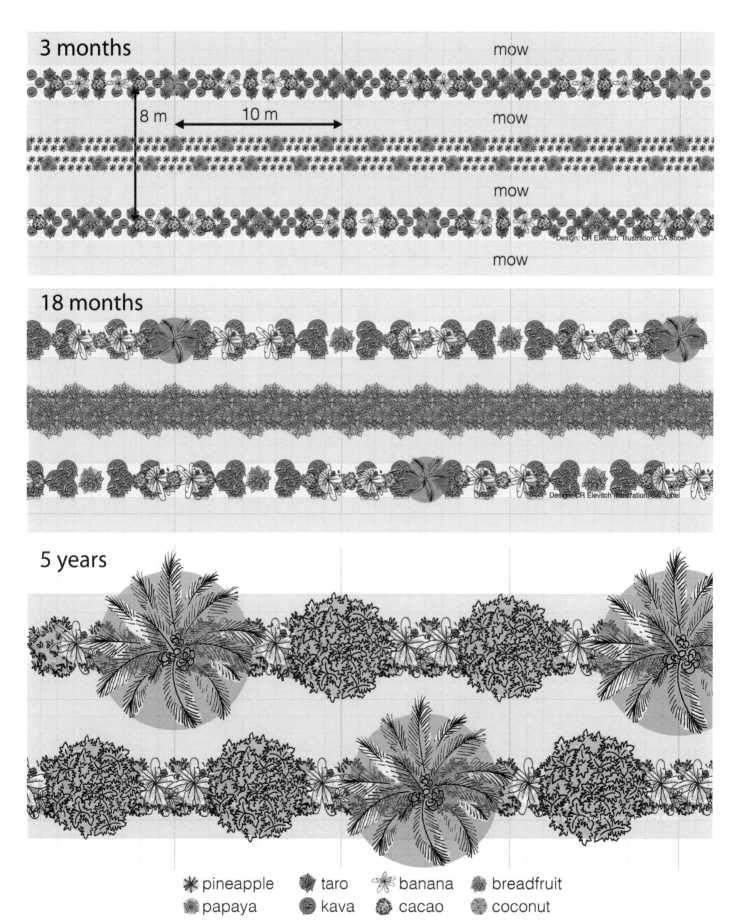

3 months

mow

8 m

10 m

mow

mow

Design: CR Elevitch Illustration: CA Sobel

mow

18 months

Design: CR Elevitch Illustration: CA Sobel

5 years

Design: CR Elevitch Illustration: CA Sobel

✳ pineapple	🍀 taro	✴ banana	🌿 breadfruit
🌸 papaya	⬤ kava	⬤ cacao	⬤ coconut

Figure 3.8 Example 1 planting layout at 3 months, 18 months, and 5 years. Initial planting density is high (see Table 3.7). Crop numbers are reduced over time as short- and medium-term crops complete their productive life cycles.

3 months

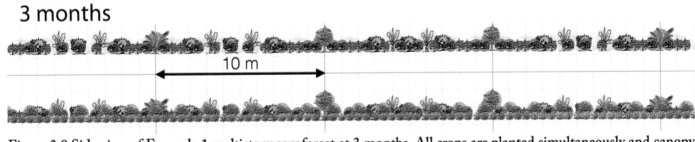

10 m

Figure 3.9 Side view of Example 1 multistory agroforest at 3 months. All crops are planted simultaneously and canopy closure is achieved within 3–4 months within the crop rows.

🌿 pineapple   🥔 taro   🌿 banana   🌳 breadfruit

🌱 papaya   🌾 kava   🌳 cacao   🌴 coconut

18 months

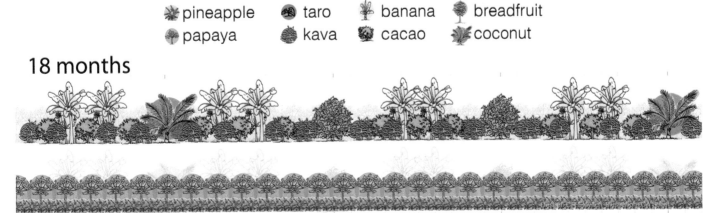

Figure 3.10 Side view of Example 1 multistory breadfruit agroforest at 18 months. At this time, the short-term taro crop has been harvested, and the banana, papaya, and pineapple have begun to produce.

5 years

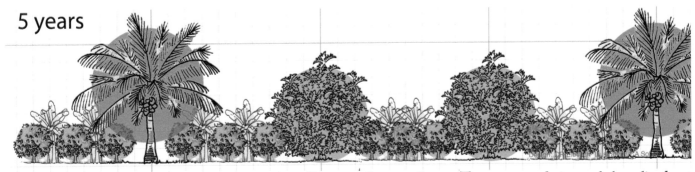

Figure 3.11 Side view of Example 1 multistory breadfruit agroforest at 5 years. The papaya and pineapple have lived out their productive lives and have been removed, the kava plants have been harvested, and the four remaining production crops are breadfruit, coconut, cacao, and banana.

Table 3.7 Example 1 crop numbers per hectare (2.5 acre) by year.

	Year 1	Year 2	Year 3	Year 4	Year 5	Year 6	Year 7	Year 8	Year 9	Year 10	notes
Banana	252	252	252	252	252	252	252	252	252	252	
Breadfruit	84	84	84	84	84	84	84	84	84	84	
Cacao	378	378	378	378	378	378	378	378	378	378	
Coconut	42	42	42	42	42	42	42	42	42	42	
Kava	1260	1260	1260	840	420	0	0	0	0	0	harvested Years 3–5
Papaya	840	840	840	840	0	0	0	0	0	0	removed in Year 4
Pineapple	10080	10080	10080	10080	0	0	0	0	0	0	removed in Year 4
Taro	1680	0	0	0	0	0	0	0	0	0	harvested Year 1

mendations found in the literature. For any specific project, spacing should be tailored to:

- Relative crop growth rates, which depend upon site conditions
- Anticipated productive lifespan of each crop
- Specific crop varieties used, which determine size, growth rate, and lifespan
- Preferred management techniques such as pruning and mowing
- Market demand for crops
- Personal preferences based on experience.

It is important to note that other crops can be substituted into this example system, which can change the timing of the crop life cycles or spacing. For this example, the site's climatic conditions are assumed to be favorable for all the crops, with annual rainfall of 2000–3000 mm (80–120 in) evenly distributed throughout the year and daytime temperatures of 21–32°C (70–90°F). Brief crop descriptions for this example are included in Table 3.5, with the canopy layers shown by year in Table 3.6.

Spacing is illustrated in Figures 3.8–11, where a 1 m × 1 m (3.3 ft × 3.3 ft) reference grid is shown. The main structural crops, breadfruit and coconut, are spaced 10 m (33 ft) apart within rows, with 8 m (26 ft) spacing between rows. Cacao are planted 2–2.5 m (6.5–8.2 ft) apart, with banana in between. Kava is planted 1–2 m (3.3–6.5 ft) from coconut and breadfruit and within the crop row.

In the space between crop rows, there is a short-term planting of pineapple in two double rows. Pineapples are planted 50 cm (20 in) apart in row, with 50 cm (20 in) between double rows. Papaya is planted within the double rows at 3 m (10 ft) spacing.

During the first year, taro grows rapidly, filling the open space around the other crops. By the end of the first year, the taro is harvested, and sold for early income generation. By this time, the other crops have grown substantially and will mostly fill the space previously occupied by the taro. Any gaps can be filled by replanting taro for a second harvest. One third of the kava plants are harvested in each of Years 3–5, which involves removing the whole plant with its root system. Where possible, the kava should be grown in prepared mounds to optimize root harvest.

The pineapple and papaya begin yielding commercial quantities in Year 2, with a productive life of about 3 years. By the time they have lived out their productive lives at the end of Year 4, the breadfruit, banana, and coconut have begun to encroach on them. This is when the pineapple and papaya are removed.

The open space between crop rows is mowed regularly or grass/weeds cut manually on steeply sloping sites (every 4 weeks, depending on rainfall). An economic analysis of Example 1 is given in Section 5.8.

4 ORCHARD ESTABLISHMENT

4.1 Site preparation

A site needs to be prepared to allow for the introduction of new plants. This includes removing or pruning back existing vegetation and preparing the soil for planting. These interventions mimic disturbances such as a hurricane or the death of a large tree, which initiate a cycle of vigorous regrowth in nature. There are usually numerous options for land preparation on any given site, and each site has its own advantages and limitations. Some general guidelines are given below, although experts on local conditions should be consulted for recommendations.

Existing vegetation. Depending on the existing vegetation, some or all plants will be removed. If possible, some vegetation should be left in place to provide wind protection and shade for working during the establishment phase. Larger desirable trees, including breadfruit trees, should be pruned back to reduce their canopy size and stimulate regrowth. Existing organic matter on the site should be preserved for use as mulch.

Soil condition. Soils should be assessed for compaction and other physical characteristics that might have been degraded by previous use. It is often beneficial to cultivate the soil surface and subsurface layers just before adding any required mineral amendments as a one-time initiative to jump start biological activity. Where soil drainage is poor, such as on compacted former plantation lands, subsurface ripping is recommended. A specially designed implement such as a Yeomans Keyline Plow[51] opens subsurface channels

---

51 Yeomans 2005

for water and root infiltration without disturbing the soil structure.

Mechanization. Mechanized mowing and tilling or other cultivation can be a cost-effective way to prepare the site if the topography and other conditions allow. Soil compaction during site preparation operations should be avoided as much as possible. Land and hole preparation should not be done if soils are saturated with water to avoid damaging the soil structure and increasing compaction. In regions where large machinery is too expensive or impractical, a range of small tilling and mowing machines is available throughout the world. Such machines can be much more economical in operation and maintenance expenses.

4.2 After site preparation

After clearing the area of unwanted vegetation and preparing the soil, planting beds should be laid out in the field and prepared. Usually, the soil receives additional cultivation within the planting beds to provide improved conditions for rapid establishment of the new planting. Mineral amendments (as determined by a soil test) and compost are added to the planting bed immediately after preparation. This is also a good time to add additional beneficial microbes such as compost tea or other homemade or commercial probiotics. The addition of active beneficial microorganisms can jump-start healthy biological activity, especially in degraded soils.

4.3 Mulch

After preparing the planting beds (or in some cases after planting), mulch is laid out to protect exposed soil from direct sun exposure and impact of rainfall. Mulch consists of fine to coarse organic material such as tree branches or grasses that is laid on top of the soil surface to hold in moisture, prevent erosion, and keep the soil cool. Mulch must be free from weed seeds, inorganic materials such as plastic, and sources of pests and diseases.

Mulch slowly breaks down to release nutrients into the soil, acting as slow release fertilizer. Additionally, it can reduce erosion caused by rainfall by up to 95% as compared to bare soil. Mulch is most effective if it lies directly in contact with the soil surface, so chopped or chipped organic material is preferable. At the interface between mulch and soil, organic activity by numerous types of soil organisms (bacteria, fungi, etc.) decomposes the mulch material, slowly releasing nutrients into the soil as a by-product of organic activity. Uncomposted organic materials should not be mixed into the soil immediately before planting, as this will create organic activity in the soil that suppresses plant growth.

4.4 Irrigation

After planting, the area should be gently soaked with water to ensure that new plants are moist and do not suffer from water stress. This will also stimulate germination of seeds that are direct sown. Daily watering during the first few days as needed during the morning or evening hours will ensure successful establishment.[52] Planting early in the wet season once the first good rains have fallen and the soil has become saturated can eliminate the need for irrigation.

Irrigation can be a wise investment in areas prone to periodic drought. Water stress can lead to loss of plant vigor and in the worst cases, failure of the planting. Installation of the irrigation system is best done immediately before or after planting, depending on planting techniques used. Low-flow irrigation systems that use either drip emitters or micro-sprinklers are most efficient at using water. If crops are planted in an area with suitably high rainfall (greater than 2000 mm/year) with only short periods of water stress, irrigation becomes less and less important as the planting becomes established. Irrigation needs are limited to only extended drought periods as root systems reach a larger and deeper soil volume.

4.5 Planting

4.5.1 Plant preparation

Breadfruit is propagated by vegetative means by root shoot, root cutting, air layer, stem cutting, grafting, or tissue culture (micropropagation), rather than from seed.[53] Breadnut is always propagated from seed. Whatever means is used to propagate the trees, they must be well cared for in the nursery so that they are healthy when planted in the field. They should also be "hardened off" before field planting by exposing them

---

52 Bornhorst 2012
53 NWC 2005; Ragone 2006, 2008; Webster 2006

to full sun for at least 2–4 weeks in the nursery to toughen them for field conditions.

Ideally, all crop plants are healthy, hardened off, and actively growing at the time of planting. This will lead to rapid establishment, helping to inhibit establishment of weeds. Avoid overgrown, top heavy planting stock that may also be root bound in containers. Such plants may no longer be actively growing, which can result in slow establishment.

4.5.2 Hole preparation

In areas that have compacted subsoil from previous land use operations, it is a good idea to dig through the subsoil before planting the breadfruit trees and other larger plants such as banana. This can be done by hand with a posthole digger or shovel, or by machine with a motorized auger. When digging in heavy clay soils, especially using an auger, the walls of the hole can be smooth, making it difficult for tree roots to emerge. In such soils, it is best to use a tool to manually cut grooves in the side of the holes where roots can push their way out of the hole. Use of biological inoculants and probiotics mixed into the soil returned to the planting hole can also help increase root penetrability.

The diameter of the hole needs to be at least up to twice as wide and as deep as the plant container. Depending on the size of the planting stock, a 30–50 cm (12–20 in) diameter hole is adequate. Some recommend a larger hole, such as 90 cm × 90 cm × 45 cm (36 in × 36 in × 18 in), but this is often unnecessary or impractical. When digging the hole, it is best to keep the soil removed from the upper soil horizon separate from the subsoil. However, when using a mechanical auger, some mixing is unavoidable.

After digging the hole, the soil gathered from the upper layer is then mixed two parts soil to one part finished compost plus mineral amendments as determined by the soil analysis. To meet organic certification requirements, these amendments may include rock phosphate, non-hydrated agricultural lime, green sand, kelp meal or a balanced commercial organic mineral amendment consistent with organic certification guidelines. The mixture of soil and amendments is then returned to the hole when planting. If mineral amendments are not available, additional compost can be added to further supplement the nutrient status in the planting bed and holes. Well prepared and amended planting holes will give plants a much more vigorous start after planting.

4.5.3 Transplanting in the field

As previously described and shown in Table 3.4, the timing of activities must be carefully staged to optimize growth outcomes. Plant materials should all be ready for planting during the establishment phase for planting simultaneously. The planting has one primary goal: to quickly fill the newly prepared area. Ideally, no gaps are left, as such areas are quickly occupied by weeds and become maintenance burdens. A few plants could be added shortly after the main planting but before the plants are rapidly growing, however, this is best kept to a minimum.

Best planting practices should always be observed. These include standard recommendations such as planting container-grown plants so that the top of the root ball is even with the soil surface. While backfilling with soil, make sure to gently firm the soil against the potting medium, thereby removing any air pockets, which can cause root dieback in the exposed area and hinder root growth.

4.6 Maintenance

The timing of maintenance activities is crucial. Failure to prune or remove plants that have matured and are ready to be displaced by other plants can result in undesirable outcomes. For example, if fast growing crops are allowed to heavily shade the young breadfruit trees, this may set back or even kill the breadfruit.

4.6.1 Weeding and control of vegetation

The greatest maintenance challenge for monocultures is to keep open space free of unwanted plants ("weeds"). The main problem with this management philosophy is that nature would like to fill any open space with vegetation. The cost of weed control is one of the biggest concerns for growers, especially those who prefer to use organic practices and do not want to use herbicides.

The best control of weeds is prevention, and the best prevention is to grow desirable plants that occupy the space that otherwise would be an open invitation to weeds. The alleys between the crop rows can be efficiently maintained by mechanical mowing. The alleys not only provide access but can be seen as areas for production of organic matter, some of which can be added to the crop rows for mulch cover and nutrients.

The space between trees within the crop rows is more challenging to keep covered with desirable vegetation. Maintaining a dense cover of crops will suppress weeds by casting shade on the ground, and occupying the root zone with a diverse array of crops. Ideally, all of these various crops and ground covers are planted after site preparation, carefully planned to include some species that will quickly cover the area and some that will persist for many years.

For weeds that come up, hand weeding and judicious use of mechanical string trimmers (brush cutters) will be necessary. If planned and implemented correctly, removing weeds will be a minor labor input. In order to maintain the canopy structure and to facilitate production, most plants within the rows will require periodic pruning. Assuming most plants are fruits, nuts, herbs, and spices, this pruning labor is required for optimal production, whether grown in an agroforest or not.

4.6.2 Pruning

In the Pacific Islands, breadfruit trees are pruned in some regions (often near homes), and allowed to grow naturally in other regions. Where trees are allowed to grow without pruning, they can easily attain heights of 12–15 m (40–50 ft) or taller. Such trees are dangerous to harvest by hand or expensive to harvest with equipment. Fruit that is mishandled or drops to the ground during harvest cannot be sold in primary commercial markets due to compromised quality and food safety regulations. In some regions, breadfruit trees are allowed to grow tall to be used as a support trellis for yam cultivation. In a configuration where cultivation of large yams takes priority over commercial requirements of breadfruit production, the breadfruit trees may be seen as primarily serving subsistence uses since the fruit is often dropped to the ground in the process of harvesting.

Pruning is essential for commercial breadfruit operations because of the inherent challenges of working with tall trees.[54] First, it greatly increases the efficiency of harvest operations to keep trees at an appropriate height (Figure 4.1). Second, the fruit is borne on new growth, so pruning both controls the size of the tree and stimulates new growth and fruiting. Third, pruning removes weak, damaged, or otherwise inopportunely positioned branches that might, for example, easily break under the weight of heavy fruit bearing. Fourth, a well-pruned breadfruit tree may suffer less damage to its main trunk and branches in high winds, allowing a quicker recovery after storm damage.

Most of the other tree crops in a multistory agroforest will also need to be pruned to optimize production and ensure that each crop receives the amount of sunlight it requires. Since most tree crops are pruned for commercial production, the pruning requirement for each crop in agroforestry may not exceed that of conventional monocultures, although the total number of trees per unit area is higher.

Pruning begins when trees are still small to achieve a favorable branch structure throughout the life of the tree. Young breadfruit trees are often topped at approximately 3 m (10 ft) in height to favor lateral branches, although some recommend a first pruning much lower to stimulate branching below 1 m (3.3 ft) in height.[55] Ideally, annual pruning is done after the end of a fruiting cycle, prior to a new growth flush.[56] The prunings can be chopped up by hand into rough material that lies relatively flat on the ground or chipped mechanically for mulch. Around the time of pruning, adding mineral amendments, mowing ground cover crops, and applying additional mulch should be carried out to ensure favorable conditions for regrowth. It is beneficial to prune when there is adequate soil moisture to allow the trees to flush out quickly, rather than wait for rain.

Pruning is a skill and art that requires professional training and experience. Proper pruning is technically challenging and can also be dangerous. When working with manual and powered saws, especially while climbing the tree, it is easy to cause injury to oneself or the tree. Safety practices include appropriate protective gear, climbing techniques, and pruning techniques. Because of the importance of pruning in a commercial fruit tree operation, especially with multiple crops in agroforestry, commercial operations

---

54 NWC 2005

55 Roberts-Nkrumah 2015
56 Elevitch et al. 2014

Figure 4.1 Pruned trees (left) can be efficiently and cost-effectively harvested. An unpruned tree (right) requires 2–3 times more time to safely pick, without climbing the tree or dropping fruit on the ground, rendering it impractical for commercial purposes.

should include staff with professional training and arborist certification to optimize pruning skills and safety practices. Where the job requires skills beyond the farmer's, a certified arborist should be hired. In addition to breadfruit management references,[57] see professional pruning references for further information.

4.7 Nutrient management

Nutrient management is a complex subject, depending upon soil characteristics, environmental effects, the structure of the crop planting, and management. Baseline knowledge of soil characteristics and available nutrients for crop growth are determined by soil testing in the site evaluation before planting (Section 3.1) and then on a recurring basis annually or whenever problems in plant vigor are observed. Recommendations for balancing nutrient availability by adding mineral and organic amendments can be determined by an expert based on the soil type and analyses. Mineral amendments can be added at the planting stage to correct deficiencies and set the planting on course for vigorous initial growth.

From an organic grower perspective, nutrient status depends upon inorganic nutrient availability together with biological activity. The addition of beneficial biological organisms can set in motion healthy biological activity in the soil and plant root zone (much like a human probiotic for the health of intestinal flora). Options for biological inoculations to jump-start organic activity include organic compost, vermicompost, compost tea,[58] Indigenous Microorganisms,[59] and Effective Microorganisms™.[60]

Once established, one may consider using conventional recommendations for nutrient amendments. Where these recommendations are given in chemical fertilizer quantities,[61] they can be converted to organically certifiable amendments based on conversion tables.[62] Conventional recommendations for nutrient additions might not be appropriate for multistory agroforestry, which is better than monocultures at retaining soluble nutrients due to a more extensive net-

57 e.g., Elevitch et al. 2014, Roberts-Nkrumah 2015

58 Radovich and Arancon 2011
59 Cho and Koyama 1997
60 Higa and Wididana 1991
61 e.g., Roberts-Nkrumah 2015
62 e.g., McLaurin and Reeves 2014

work of root systems and higher organic activity that can uptake nutrients before they are carried away by water. When growing many different types of plants together, there are complex biological dynamics between plants and soil, which cannot be directly compared with the dynamics of monocultures.

Therefore, nutrient management is best customized to the orchards based upon regular soil and plant tissue tests for nutrient status, in addition to real-time observations of plant health by the grower. Rather than relying upon standard formulas or guesswork, such testing can give direct insight into nutrient status.

4.8 Pests and diseases

While breadfruit is generally considered to be a relatively pest and disease-free tree, several fungal diseases, including *Fusarium*, *Phytophthora*, and fruit *Anthracnose* have been found on breadfruit trees. These usually do not cause serious problems, as long as the trees are healthy and good air circulation is maintained around and under the canopy. Proper sanitation should be carried out by removing fallen fruit from the area. Holistic, regenerative practices to improve soil microbial biodiversity, such as growing appropriate ground covers and application of prepared microbial inoculants and compost teas, can help mitigate the impact of disease organisms.

Pests such as fruit fly, white fly, scale, and mealy bugs may not be a problem for local markets as they usually cause only minor damage, but in some cases, especially when trees are stressed by drought and neglect, mealy bugs can be a serious problem.[63] Fruit flies will pose a problem for export of fresh fruit to most markets and approved postharvest treatment will be necessary.[64]

Sunburn on fruit (which leads to browning and rotting) can occur at some times of the year. A multistory agroforest which provides a light canopy over the breadfruit can help keep temperatures down and possibly reduce issues with sunburn on the fruit.

Decline and death of trees from *Phellinus noxius*, a fungal organism, have been reported from several Pacific Islands and plant parasitic nematodes have been recorded in many tropical areas, including Hawaii and other Pacific Islands.[65] As these and other disease organisms are associated with roots, but cannot be seen with the naked eye, it is essential to be cautious and follow good sanitation practices when sharing propagating material, especially roots and young plants grown from root cuttings or root shoots. While state and national plant quarantine guidelines and required plant import/export permits and phytosanitary inspections and permits are often considered to be a hassle, they exist to help provide biosecurity and prevent the spread of invasive species, pests, and diseases. These rules need to be followed when sharing propagating material across regional and international borders to help prevent the spread of potentially devastating pests and diseases. A major advantage of planting micropropagated breadfruit trees produced by a licensed horticultural facility is that the plants are carefully screened for disease (also called disease indexing) and can be certified free of fungi, bacteria, nematodes, and viruses.

4.9 Example 2: Monoculture conversion

Many growers may benefit from converting a mature monoculture planting of breadfruit or breadnut into a multistory agroforest. The benefits include all the advantages of agroforestry described in Section 1.5 such as greater total income and profits per unit area and spreading market risks over additional crops. It is best to start a breadfruit agroforest with young breadfruit trees from the outset, but retrofitting a monoculture of breadfruit is also feasible.

The Breadfruit Research Orchard at McBryde Garden, National Tropical Botanical Garden, Kauai, Hawaii was incrementally converted to an agroforest beginning in August 2017 and is used for this example. In brief, this orchard consists of several cultivars of breadfruit and a section of breadnut trees (which will be the focus of this example) growing in a primarily grassy, mowed lawn. The spacing between breadfruit/breadnut trees is 10–12 m (33–40 ft) between trees and rows (see aerial photo Figure 4.2). A comprehensive assessment of this site is included in Table 4.1.

4.9.1 Planning

Planning for retrofitting a monoculture is similar to planning for starting an agroforest from an open site,

---

63 Redfern 2007
64 see e.g., NWC 2005

65 Lau 2017

Table 4.1 Example 2 site evaluation (NTBG McBryde Garden Breadfruit Research Orchard). This site is used as an example of converting a breadfruit monoculture into a multistory agroforest in Section 4.9.

General site description	This gently sloping 0.53 ha (1.3 ac) site lies in Lawai Valley in McBryde Garden of the National Tropical Botanical Garden
Property map (location, dimensions, etc.)	 Left: An aerial photo of the Breadfruit Research Orchard. Right: A topographic map of the orchard with the breadfruit and breadnut trees marked with green circles.
Location	The site is located in the ahupua'a of Lāwa'i on Kaua'i Island. GPS coordinates are (21.900546, -159.507168).
Topography	The site slopes gently to the southwest.
Elevation	Approximately 30 m (100 ft) above sea level.
Wind	This site is impacted by seasonally significant winds that swirl through the valley.
Soil	<table><tr><th>Map Unit Symbol</th><th>Map Unit Name</th><th>Acres</th></tr><tr><td>HnA</td><td>Hanalei silty clay, 0–2% slopes</td><td>1.0</td></tr><tr><td>PkB</td><td>Pohakupu silty clay loam, 0–8% slopes</td><td>0.3</td></tr><tr><td>**Totals for Area of Interest**</td><td></td><td>**1.3**</td></tr></table> The soils are classified as prime farmland, with HnA considered to have poor drainage, so flooding can be damaging to crops. Soils map source: https://websoilsurvey.nrcs.usda.gov/app/WebSoilSurvey.aspx

Table 4.1 Example 2 site evaluation (NTBG McBryde Garden Breadfruit Research Orchard) (cont.)

Annual rainfall	**Mean Monthly Rainfall (mm)** Rainfall Atlas of Hawai'i 2011, University of Hawai'i ☐ Map: 21.905° N, 159.494° W ☐ Station: East Lawai A bar chart showing mean monthly rainfall from Jan to Dec, with values ranging approximately between 100 and 180 mm, y-axis marked 0, 50, 100, 150, 200. Mean Annual Rainfall: 1386.9 mm Data from nearest station on Hawaii Interactive Rainfall map (Giambelluca et al. 2013)
Weather (historic averages, extreme events)	The mean annual rainfall in the region is about 1370 mm (54 inches) per year, with winter months moderately moister than summer months. Temperatures are in the range 16–30°C (60–85°F). Three major hurricanes have hit Kauai since 1959 (Dot 1959, Iwa 1982, Iniki 1992).
History of uses	An area of Hawaiian settlement, the site was in sugarcane cultivation by the early 1900s and remained so until the late 1960s In 1970 it became part of NTBG.
Description of present condition	The site is a well maintained breadfruit orchard of trees planted in 2004 and 2006, with mowed grass ground cover. The grass has been removed and mulch added within the drip line.
Existing vegetation/cover types	The ground cover is mixed grasses including invasive Guinea grass (*Megathyrsus maximus*) and several low-growing creeping grasses, and wedelia (*Wedelia fructicosa*).
Existing vegetation health and function	The breadfruit trees have been well maintained and are in good health.
Water resources	Lawai Stream flows through the Garden, approximately 150 m (500 ft) from the site. The Luawai Reservoir is located immediately above the ridge adjacent to the project site and this water is the source of the agricultural water available to McBryde Garden.
Historical resources	On the immediate site, there are no known historical resources.
Cultural resources	This is a highly visible site with potential to expose garden visitors to breadfruit cultivation in Pacific Island cultural context as well as an example of regeneration of former plantation lands.
Existing wildlife and their impact	A number of bird species inhabit the surrounding area. Aside from feral chickens and pigs, there is little impact on the site.
Threatened and endangered species	Nene have rarely been observed landing in the big field adjacent and gallinules near the stream crossover, but never across the road.
Recreational and aesthetic values	This site is a very visible part of McBryde Garden's well-known living collections. It is viewed by thousands of visitors each year.
Existing roads and access	Located along the main road in the garden. Also accessible by foot from tour drop off station near "Food for Thought."
Utilities	There is no access to electricity, although agricultural water is present.
Zoning restrictions	See Kauai County records.
Environmental threats (disease, pests, etc.)	Feral pigs are present in the surrounding area. Feral chickens are also present in large numbers. This site is freely accessible to Garden visitors, therefore any poisonous or otherwise hazardous plants should be avoided.
Activities on neighboring properties	Immediately to the east above the ridge, Kauai Coffee Company has its plantation and agricultural reservoir.

except that the spacing between the breadfruit trees (and other existing plants that are to remain) is already determined, which in turn affects crop selection and the rest of the crop spacing. For ease of management, the new crops are planted in rows along the breadnut tree rows (Figure 4.2). This technique allows the establishment of all the new crops in a prepared planting bed 1.2 m (4 ft) wide, while the open space between rows can be mowed efficiently when necessary.

In this example, the portion of the orchard of interest consists of breadnut trees, which have a more upright form and more open canopy than breadfruit trees. With a canopy density of about 50% (letting half of the sunlight through), a range of long-term shade tolerant crops were planted including cacao, coffee, vanilla, black pepper, and cardamom. Medium-term crops included banana and the native Hawaiian shrub mamaki (*Pipturus kauaiensis*), which is used for its medicinal properties. Short-term crops consisted of a dense planting of vegetables including lettuces, kale, beans, eggplant, chili pepper, and many more. Within

rows, three-dimensional space was planned to be occupied by productive plants that are maintained by hand, but with various yields that more than offset maintenance costs (Figure 4.3 and Table 4.2).

Between the tree/crop rows, the open space was planted with cover crops to greatly increase organic matter production compared with the existing slow-growing grasses. These included buckwheat (for very fast cover), Sunn hemp, and sunflower. For long-term cover and organic matter production, pigeon pea, gliricidia, ice cream bean, kukui, and other fast growing trees will be planted and pruned regularly. In addition to organic matter production, the planting between rows gives wind protection to the crop rows, which is an important benefit on this site.

4.9.2 Site preparation

New plantings will have difficulty establishing within an established tree orchard with ground cover unless the site is prepared to admit them. In this example, the trees were first pruned back to open up the canopy and stimulate regrowth (Figures 4.4–4.5). Second, the

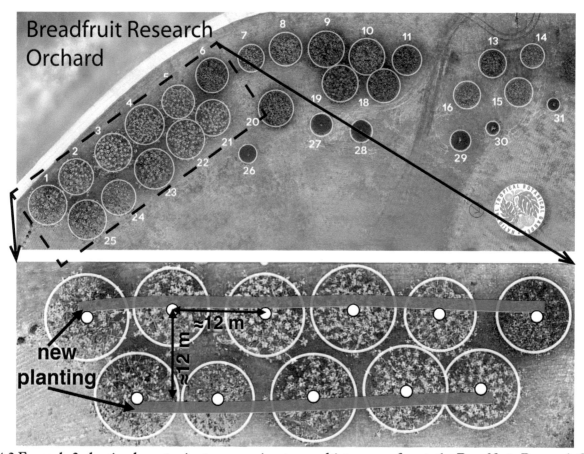

Figure 4.2 Example 2 planting layout prior to conversion to a multistory agroforest, the Breadfruit Research Orchard at McBryde Garden, National Tropical Botanical Garden, Kauai, Hawaii (see Table 4.1 for site assessment).

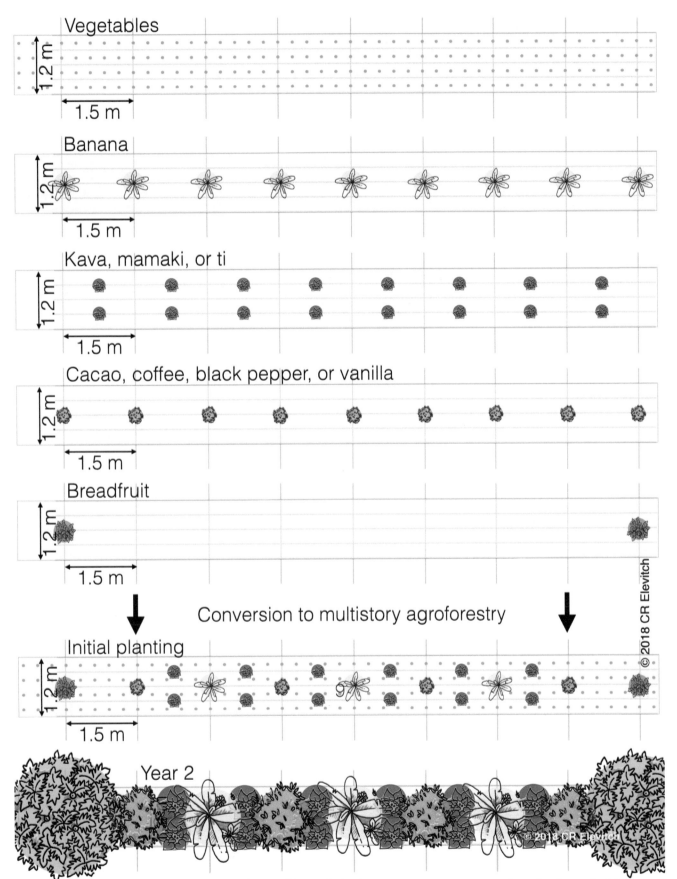

Vegetables

1.2 m

1.5 m

Banana

1.2 m

1.5 m

Kava, mamaki, or ti

1.2 m

1.5 m

Cacao, coffee, black pepper, or vanilla

1.2 m

1.5 m

Breadfruit

1.2 m

1.5 m

Conversion to multistory agroforestry

© 2018 CR Elevitch

Initial planting

1.2 m

1.5 m

Year 2

© 2018 CR Elevitch

Figure 4.3 In converting a monoculture such as in Example 2, the existing tree rows were densely planted with crops that rapidly grow into a multistory agroforest. Spacing for the crops can be determined from monoculture spacing as shown in the top five monoculture crop rows illustrated here. Combining the top five rows into one planting as illustrated in the sixth row initiates the new agroforest.

Figure 4.4 Example 2 initial field planting. Top left: Breadnut orchard prior to planting. Top right: Heavy pruning of breadnut trees in preparation for planting. Middle left: All tree prunings were chipped for mulch. Middle right: Crop row beds were dug by hand and using an auger. Bottom left: After digging and addition of soil amendments, crop rows were mulched and irrigation drip lines laid out. Bottom right: The crop beds were planted densely with crops and buckwheat as a quick cover crop.

Figure 4.5 Example 2 growth over the first six months. Top left: Early coverage primarily is by the quick-growing vegetables and other ground covers. Top right: After about 4 months, the early vegetables are now harvested, leaving the longer term vegetables and crops. Middle left: At the onset of seasonal rains, the space between rows was planted with a cover crop of buckwheat, Sunn hemp, and sunflower for organic matter production and to enhance beneficial biological activity. Bottom left: After 6 months, a multistory agroforest begins to be apparent. Bottom right: Short-term crops harvested within the first 6 months generate net income that helps offset the cost of establishment.

Table 4.2 Example 2 crop numbers per 12 m × 1.2 m (40 × 4 ft) crop row by year.

	Year 1	Year 2	Year 3	Year 4	Year 5	Year 6	Year 7	Year 8	Year 9	Year 10	notes
Banana	3	3	3	3	3	3	3	3	3	3	
Breadnut	2	2	2	2	2	2	2	2	2	2	
Cacao, coffee, vanilla, black pepper, or cardamom	4	4	4	4	4	4	4	4	4	4	
Mamaki	12	12	12	12	12	12	12	12	12	12	
Vegetables	160	40	0	0	0	0	0	0	0	0	Harvested within 18 months

well-established ground cover under the trees was removed where new crops were to be planted. This is especially needed in areas where soil compaction has taken place over a period of years. Once the soil has been loosened up mechanically, additions of mineral amendments (determined through recommendations based upon soil analysis) and well-cured compost were added and either be top-dressed or turned in. Finally, the exposed soil was covered with organic matter immediately after preparation to reduce the negative impacts of direct sun and dessication.

Conditions created by pruning and ground preparation allow establishment of new crops in close proximity to existing trees. Pruning existing trees also has the important effect of slowing transpiration (loss of moisture through foliage), reducing the draw on available soil moisture. Mulching and soil amendment along the planting rows further enhances regrowth and the new plantings.

In one area of the orchard, with young breadfruit trees planted in 2016, a no-till approach was implemented. Grass in the areas surrounding the trees was allowed to grow to 12–15 inches then mowed and the area direct seeded with a mix of buckwheat, Sunn hemp, sunflower, vetch (*Vicia sativa*), and clover (*Trifolium* spp.).

4.9.3 Crop succession and maintenance

A dense planting of early crops will generate early income, suppress weed growth, and enhance conditions for long-term crops. Assuming that this initial planting within crop rows establishes successfully, most "maintenance" activities will consist of crop care and harvesting. Little space is available for weed establishment, so only light weeding will be needed. In other words, weed control is replaced by crop production activities (Figure 4.4).

The density of short-term crop planting should be balanced with available labor and markets. Where one or both of these is a limiting factor, cover crops and permanent ground covers can be planted instead of crops. In this case, the labor of maintaining, harvesting, and distributing crops can be reduced, however, there will be no short-term returns.

When growing short-, medium-, and long-term crops together as shown in Figure 4.3, the timing of crop maintenance activities is critical. This usually requires removing or pruning back crops as they begin to hinder, rather than facilitate, the development of neighboring crops. For example, young cacao trees thrive in the shade of surrounding crops, but their production will be diminished if shade levels are too high as the trees mature. Therefore, management decisions to prune or remove earlier crops must be made in real-time in order to facilitate an advantageous succession from crop to crop.

5 PRODUCTS AND COMMERCIAL MARKETS

5.1 Fresh fruit

Breadfruit is an extremely versatile food, and the fresh fruit can be used at all stages of development and prepared in many ways.[66] It is most commonly harvested and consumed when mature, but still firm, and used as a starchy staple (see Table 2.5). As with most starchy staple crops, breadfruit is relatively bland and

---

66 Ragone 2011

can form the basis for an array of dishes, taking on the flavor of other ingredients in the dish. Very small young fruit, 2.5–6 cm (1–2.5 in) or larger in diameter, can be boiled and have a flavor similar to that of artichoke hearts. These can be pickled or marinated. Certain local and export markets (such as expatriate Pacific and Caribbean islanders living in temperate regions where breadfruit does not grow) require fresh fruit especially for preparing breadfruit in traditional ways.[67]

Mature and almost mature breadfruit can be steamed or boiled and substituted for potato in many recipes. Ripe fruit are sweet and used to make pies, cakes and other desserts.[68] Consumers, chefs, and food processors in breadfruit growing regions are expanding the culinary uses of the fruit at home, in restaurants and with street vendors (Figure 5.1). Building upon time-honored methods of preparation, such as roasting the fruit on a fire, pounding it into a poi-like form, or cooking it with coconut cream, breadfruit is now being used to make appetizers, snacks, baked goods, beverages, desserts, main dishes, and more.

5.2 Processed products

Processing mature and ripe fruit into shelf-stable products, such as chips and other snacks, fries, beverages such as "vegan milk," beer and liqueurs, dips, fruit bars, baked goods, and other value-added products, is fundamental to greater utilization of the fruit and expanding markets.

Steamed or roasted mature fruit can be minimally processed—sliced, vacuum packed, and frozen—and sold in local markets in Hawaii and the Caribbean, as well as exported to U.S. markets from the Caribbean. Mature and ripe fruit can also be mashed into a dough, vacuum packed, and frozen for further use. The dough can form the base for flat breads, pizza, pie crust, and as a flat noodle substitute. Semi-anaerobic fermentation can transform mature starchy fruit into a long-lasting slightly acidic doughy form.

Figure 5.1 Fresh fruit sold directly to restaurants or consumers can fetch the highest price per unit weight, but must also be of prime quality for discerning customers.

Breadfruit flour and flour-based value-added products have been gaining attention in recent years. Flour provides a simple and effective means to deal with fruit perishability. Any cultivar can be dried and made into flour at the firm, mature stage, and it can be done using raw or parboiled slices, peeled or unpeeled, with or without the core. Basic guidelines to drying breadfruit and grinding it into flour have been produced by the Ministry of Agriculture in Guyana,[69] Compatible Technology International,[70] Trees That Feed Foundation[71] and the Breadfruit Institute/UBCO.[72]

'Ma'afala' has significant advantages for processing into high quality flour in that it contains 7.6% protein compared to 'Yellow' (5.3%) and 'White' (4.1%).[73] Depending upon the cultivar, protein content of the flour ranges from 1.8% to 7.6%, averaging 3.1%. Protein content (DW) of fresh fruit ranges from 2.8% to 6.2%, averaging 3.9%. Breadnut seed flour contains 13.1% protein. The fact that breadfruit and the resulting flour are gluten free has immense appeal to consumers, chefs, and entrepreneurs. Potential demand and

67 NWC 2005
68 See Ragone et al. 2012, Breadfruit Institute https://ntbg.org/breadfruit/food/recipes

69 NARI 2010
70 CTI 2012
71 TTFF 2015
72 Breadfruit Institute/UBCO 2016
73 Jones et al. 2011

uses for breadfruit flour greatly expands and complements existing and potential markets for fresh fruit and value-added products. Generally Recognized as Safe (GRAS) status for flour made from breadfruit flesh was approved in 2016.[74]

Producers of breadfruit flour and other value-added products will need to use facilities that comply with the United States FDA Food Safety Modernization Act or equivalent regulations in other countries to ensure food safety. Those who would like to export to the United States will also need to register food production facilities in compliance with the "Public Health Security and Bioterrorism Preparedness and Response Act of 2002 (the Bioterrorism Act)."

5.3 Crop portfolio

As with many indigenous crops, breadfruit's potential as a staple food has been greatly underestimated for many decades. In recent years, creative chefs, processors, and entrepreneurs around the world have demonstrated its extreme flexibility for use in numerous dishes, both starchy and sweet, as well as a range of processed products as described above. Breadfruit's versatility is only limited by the imagination.

There are numerous general references available for developing and marketing agricultural crops.[75] From the perspective of breadfruit in agroforestry, our analysis focuses on opportunities to look at breadfruit products in the context of a suite of crops, called here a crop portfolio (Figure 5.2). Ideally, the crop portfolio is a perfect match for the multistory agroforest (which includes crops from several different canopy layers yielding over a series of time frames), the growing environment, and the personal preferences of the producers. Just as with investment portfolios, crop portfolios can reduce the overall risks of farming. As market demand and prices vary up and down, it is likely that some of the crops in a portfolio will remain profitable, whereas others may cost more to produce than the price received. Similarly, as weather conditions change from year to year, chances are that some of the crops will thrive, while others may suffer excessively from extreme events such as droughts and gale-force winds. As a whole, a crop portfolio is usu-

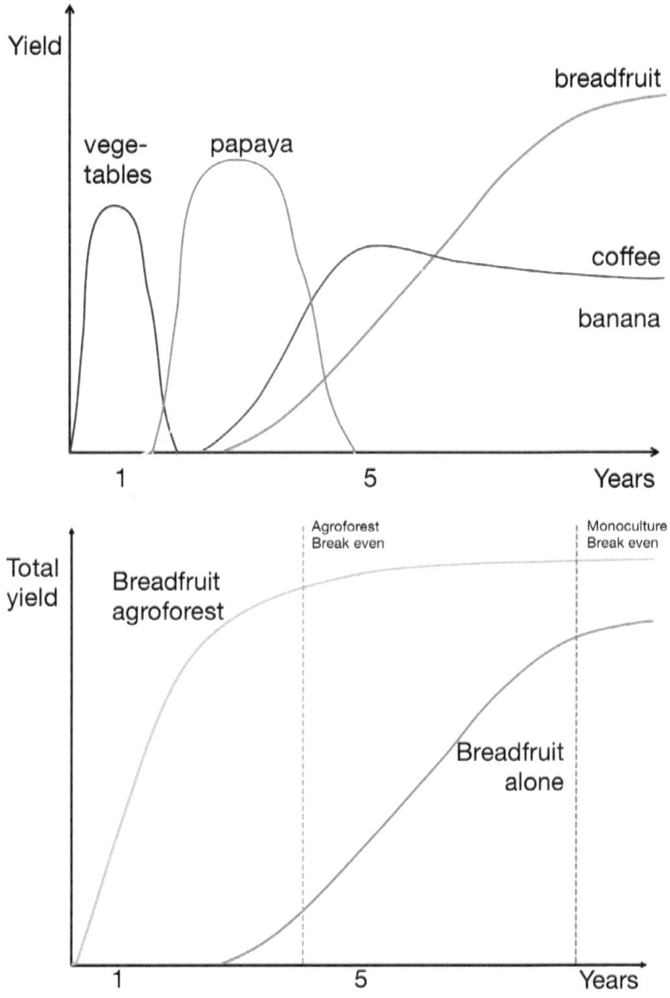

Figure 5.2 Top: Conceptual crop portfolio yield curves for short-, medium-, and long-term crops grown simultaneously in a breadfruit agroforest. Bottom: Comparative total yields and break-even on investment for a breadfruit agroforest and breadfruit grown in a monoculture. Not only can total yields be significantly greater in an agroforest, but break-even can be achieved much earlier.

ally less susceptible to risks and more profitable than any single crop.

5.4 Markets

The term "market" refers to a group of buyers with common interests and requirements. Although there are substantial export markets for fresh and processed breadfruit,[76] we focus on local markets here because throughout the world, local food systems and food security are high priorities. As a highly productive and nutritious staple crop, breadfruit is well suited to addressing local issues around food production. Of

74 USDA FDA 2016
75 e.g., Elevitch and Love 2013

76 NWC 2005; Webster 2006; Roberts-Nkrumah 2015; McGregor and Stice 2018

course, much of this discussion, such as the cash flow analysis as calculated below, can be used for both local and export markets.

Since breadfruit is relatively new in commercial markets in many regions even where it was traditionally an important staple, comparison with markets for similar staples may give guidance regarding market demand. For example, taro consumption in New Zealand may be a useful benchmark for predicting the scale of the local breadfruit market, which is estimated to be roughly a third as large as the taro market.[77] Another comparable staple is white potato. A public marketing campaign[78] in Hawaii suggested that breadfruit is an excellent substitute for imported potato, and superior in flavor and nutrition.[79] It is conceivable that breadfruit could replace a significant percentage of the approximately 23 million kg (50 million lb) of white potato imported to Hawaii yearly.

Currently in many production regions, breadfruit is most commonly seen in farmers markets, certain retail locations, and on innovative restaurant menus. As awareness increases among consumers and production increases on farms, one can expect breadfruit markets to significantly expand in all categories of produce markets including:

- Wholesale distributors
- Processors
- Retailers
- Restaurants
- Consumers.

The most successful growers sell to two or three of these markets to ensure that they can sell all of their produce at the highest price possible. Selling to a wholesale distributor or processor is usually the lowest price point, but is a good option during the peak production seasons when other markets cannot absorb the amount of breadfruit available. Prices during peak season may be lower than the cost of production, however, such income can make the combined economic returns profitable.

Selling directly to retailers, restaurants, or consumers will command higher prices than distributors or processors, but involves the additional work of taking orders and often delivery. Excess, damaged or by-product fruit from processing can be sold for animal feed or fermented anaerobically for extended storage periods.

One can expect that certified organic produce will usually fetch a higher price when offered to health- or environmental-values-conscious consumers. During peak harvest times, certified organic produce may not receive a higher price than conventional, although it may still have the advantage in the marketplace among discerning customers.

5.5 Complementary crops

With good planning, the suite of crops in a multistory breadfruit agroforest can be leveraged to provide several advantages from cost and marketing perspectives. These advantages include:

Expanding sales to existing customers. Customers who already purchase a grower's breadfruit, especially if it is high quality, will often be interested in purchasing other produce or products, expanding income opportunities with existing customers.

Expanding customer base. Additional products expand the customer base to those who were not originally interested in breadfruit, but may become interested at some time in the future.

Sharing postharvest handling and distribution infrastructure (aka "enterprise stacking"). Much of the infrastructure set up for breadfruit can be dedicated to other crops, increasing returns on infrastructure investments.

More efficient use of labor and facilities. Because of the seasonality of breadfruit, other crops allow productive use of labor and facilities during the pauses in breadfruit harvest, which can be several weeks or months. Making consistent use of production capacity throughout the year can greatly increase farm efficiency.

Processed products. For producers who also make processed products, complementary crops can be selected that are potential co-ingredients. For production of dessert products, complementary fruits, spices, and other flavorings can be included in the crop portfolio. Similarly, crops that can share processing equipment or know-how are advantageous.

77 NWC 2005
78 Breadfruit vs. Potato https://hawaiihomegrown.org/breadfruit-vs-potato
79 Ragone et al. 2016

Expand food choices for home consumption. Small family farms can offset food purchases for home consumption by growing what they prefer to eat within their breadfruit agroforest. This can amount to a significant savings in the family food budget.

5.6 Value-added

Many associate the concept of "value-added" only with processing. However, adding value can take place at any stage of growing, harvest, handling, labeling, and processing (Figure 5.3). For the purposes of this guide, value-added refers to imparting characteristics or qualities to a product that differentiate it from a generic commodity and enhance its value in the marketplace.[80] Viewed from this perspective, the value of a grower's product can be increased in many different ways to gain advantages in the marketplace. In practice, the most successful farmers do not sell their product on the generic market, but add value in several of these ways.

For breadfruit, some of the ways value can be added are listed below. These begin at the time of planting the trees, and continue throughout the life of the agroforest.

Cultivars planted. Certain cultivars are better for certain markets. For example, a cultivar such as 'Ma'afala' has a relatively small-sized fruit, which is an appropriate size for small families as a fresh fruit, but more work for certain processed products. The converse is true for a large-fruited cultivar such as 'Otea'. The lesson here is to select cultivars that are well-suited for planned markets.

Tree care/health. Mulching, pruning, irrigation (where and when needed), enhancing soil nutrition, etc., will promote healthy tree growth and high quality fruit. This extends to other areas of the farm operations. For example, in windy areas, growing windbreaks for breadfruit trees will reduce fruit damage from the wind.

Harvest care. Harvesting fruit at optimum maturity for the intended uses is crucial for breadfruit. A firm, mature fruit is ideal for most culinary uses, and anything less or more mature is not favored by consumers. For other uses, such as chips and fries, a slightly less mature fruit is favored. Harvest techniques that avoid

Figure 5.3 Adding value can take place at any stage of production, from tree care and harvest, to handling, processing, and branding.

scuffing or bruising fruit also ensure highest quality fruit for the marketplace.

Postharvest handling. After harvesting, care in transport and storage help retain fruit quality and extend shelf life by up to 2 weeks.[81] Sorting and grading ensure that the highest quality fruit go to the highest paying and most appropriate markets. Some markets, such as export markets for fresh fruit, require rigorous grading standards.[82]

Certifications. For virtually all mainstream commercial markets (wholesale, retail, etc.), food safely regulations should be observed and well documented.[83] Organic certifications add value in the eyes of consumers who are conscious of their own health and environmental health. These consumers are willing to pay more for certified organic produce. In many regions, there are also certifications for locally grown. The prospect of a regenerative organic certification is promising for agroforestry (see Section 5.7).

Processing. Processing into products is the last stage in the value-added sequence (Figures 5.4–5.5). This is also where the farm business expands into new businesses with their own range of requirements for handling, facilities and equipment, food safety regulations, storage, shipping, etc.

---

80 Elevitch and Love 2013

81 Elevitch et al. 2014
82 NWC 2005
83 see e.g., Produce Safety Alliance (n.d.); CTAHR (n.d.)

5.7 Regenerative organic agroforestry certification

Recognizing the risks of the degradation of soils and environmental services due to agriculture, there is increasing interest in agricultural practices that regenerate soil and biodiversity.[84] Regenerative agriculture is a term used to describe systems that go beyond only sustaining the status quo ("sustainable") to those that improve agricultural conditions over time. Regarding regenerative agricultural systems, a major organic research organization[85] reports, "Regenerative organic agriculture is marked by tendencies towards closed nutrient loops, greater diversity in the biological community, fewer annuals and more perennials, and greater reliance on internal rather than external resources." These characteristics correspond well with those of agroforestry. "Regenerative organic agroforestry" is a natural extension of the more general practice of regenerative organic agriculture. Breadfruit is a prime candidate for use in and demonstration of regenerative organic agroforestry because it has successfully been grown in agroforests for millennia with many benefits as outlined in the preceding sections.

Recently, a regenerative organic certification standard was proposed in order to distinguish regenerative practices from certified organic practices.[86] Regenerative Organic Certification is a holistic agriculture certification encompassing practices that follow rigorous criteria:

- Increase soil organic matter over time and sequester atmospheric carbon in that soil
- Improve animal welfare on farms
- Provide economic stability and fair labor conditions for workers
- Create environmentally and economically resilient production ecosystems and communities.

Such a certification would conceivably help farmers differentiate their products in the marketplace to appeal to customers who would like to support practices with a greater scope of benefits than those allowed under traditional organic agricultural labels. In order to reach this values-based consumer market, a new certification for regenerative agroforestry may be a means for environmental-values-oriented customers to financially reward farmers for providing soil and water conservation, biodiverse wildlife habitat, and other benefits for the environment and human communities. Table 5.1 lists characteristics of agroforestry practices that should be supported in a regenerative organic agroforestry certification program.

Organic certification programs such as USDA Organic, Demeter®, and others allow for agroforestry practices, but they do not distinguish between the benefits of annual and perennial crops, monocultures and polycultures, and other important features that set agroforestry apart from other agriculture. Other certifications such as Rainforest Alliance and UTZ focus more on social benefits and supply chain traceability than on cultivation and environmental services. The

Table 5.1 Important characteristics of agroforestry that yield multiple environmental benefits and that are not required by current organic certifications.

Agroforestry characteristics	Benefits/advantages
Perennial	Deep rooted, more tolerant of weather extremes, low input once established
Multistory, multistrata	Optimize light interception, diverse root systems for nutrient capture, retaining moisture, wind resistance, more pleasant working conditions
Successional plant communities	Supports natural regeneration (internal processes rather than inputs), trajectories to production or conservation systems
Analog to natural forest ecosystems	Proven track record of sustainability, regeneration; cultivating natural systems that accommodate desired yields and services
Crop/plant/biome biodiversity	Reduced risk from environmental and economic disturbances
Environmental services designed into system	Soil and water conservation, carbon sequestration, etc.

84 Leakey 2014
85 Rodale Institute 2014; www.regenorganic.org
86 NSF International 2017; www.regenorganic.org

Figure 5.4 A wide range of shelf-stable products can be made from breadfruit. Clockwise from upper left: Steamed, frozen, and vacuum packed pieces of mature fruit; fries, which can also be frozen and packaged; fried chips with various flavorings (including center photo); baked goods such as muffins and cookies; flour premixed with other ingredients for home cooking; and pure breadfruit flour for use in baking or cooking.

Figure 5.5 Clockwise from upper left: Beer brewed in part with breadfruit; pies made with a base of ripe breadfruit; marinated young breadfruit; various flavored drinks and preserves; distilled liqueur; breakfast cereal made with breadfruit as a base; flavored dips (center photo).

lack of certifications specifically for agroforestry suggests an opening to consider the possibilities for how regenerative organic certification might be configured for breadfruit agroforestry. As there currently are no agroforestry certifications, this guide recommends techniques and amendments consistent with current organic certifications such as USDA Organic.

5.8 Economic evaluation

All commercial farm enterprises should be based upon economic projections of costs and returns over time. Agroforestry systems are more complicated to evaluate economically than monocultures due to multiple income streams from various crops over differing time periods, with their related but diverse costs of establishment, maintenance, and harvest. Additionally, agroforestry has numerous benefits that are difficult to quantify economically, such as long-term soil improvement, risk reduction, etc. In some countries, additional financial benefits may also be derived from resource conservation subsidies and carbon credits, such as USDA EQIP funding in the United States and its associated island states in the Pacific and Caribbean.

There are several approaches to economic evaluation including enterprise budgeting, cashflow analysis, evaluation of economic indicators (e.g., Net Present Value) and cost of production analysis.[87] In the following example analysis of Example 1 (Section 3.7), cashflow analysis is highlighted (Figure 5.6). Cashflow analysis accounts for expense and income streams over the life of the project. This type of analysis is well suited for agroforestry because it allows for multiple enterprises (crops, products, etc.) simultaneously and incorporating different time frames is straightforward.

Table 5.2 Example 1 costs common to all crops per hectare (2.5 ac). Estimated expenses are given for Hawaii, one of the more expensive places to do business in the world.

	Year 1	Year 2	Year 3	Year 4	Year 5	Year 6	Year 7	Year 8	Year 9	Year 10
Establishment										
Site preparation (vegetation removal, tilling, etc.)	$5,000									
Secure site perimeter	$2,500									
Early maintenance	$3,000									
Organic matter (mulch)	$2,000									
Cover crops	$1,000									
Soils										
Analysis	$350	$350	$350	$350	$350	$350	$350	$350	$350	$350
Amendments (mineral, biological, etc.)	$1,500	$500	$500	$500	$500	$500	$500	$500	$500	$500
Labor	$800	$400	$400	$400	$400	$400	$400	$400	$400	$400
Irrigation										
Installation	$3,500									
Water	$1,000	$500	$500	$500	$500	$500	$500	$500	$500	$500
Maintenance labor	$400	$400	$400	$400	$400	$400	$400	$400	$400	$400
Periodic pest and disease control										
Materials	$300	$300	$300	$300	$300	$300	$300	$300	$300	$300
Labor	$400	$400	$400	$400	$400	$400	$400	$400	$400	$400
Weed control										
In row (hand labor)	$2,000	$2,000	$2,000	$2,000	$2,000	$2,000	$2,000	$2,000	$2,000	$2,000
Between rows (tractor)	$4,800	$4,800	$4,800	$4,800	$4,800	$4,800	$4,800	$4,800	$4,800	$4,800
Totals	$28,550	$9,650	$9,650	$9,650	$9,650	$9,650	$9,650	$9,650	$9,650	$9,650

87 Fleming et al. 2009, Godsey 2010

For this example we consider typical fixed and variable costs in the operation of the agroforest presented in Example 1. Expenses are broken down into two categories:

- Common costs for all crops (Table 5.2)
- Costs directly related to individual crops (Tables 5.5–5.7).

Income streams are broken down by crop based on crop numbers and estimated yield per plant (Tables 5.3–5.4, 5.8–5.9). The difference between total expenses and total income is the cash flow (Tables 5.10).

5.8.1 Caveats to this analysis

Expense and income values are based on estimated yields in favorable growing environments from the literature and typical pricing at wholesale in Hawaii. Price estimates are also based on the local Hawaii certified organic market, which is higher value than many other markets in the world. Actual numbers are quite variable depending on the environments and markets. The numbers presented here should be seen as an example for creating an economic budget for a specific project. Also, this analysis does not include

farm overhead costs such as land cost, the cost of borrowing money, insurance, access, utilities, etc. Moreover, it does not include farm manager compensation or profits for future investment or to offset potential future losses. These amounts, in addition to the initial establishment costs, will need to be covered by the positive "cash flow" projected in the analysis.

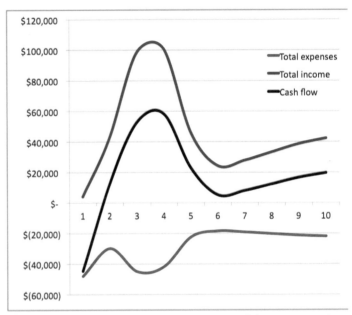

Figure 5.6 Example 1 cashflow estimate (Tables 5.3–10).

Table 5.3 Example 1 crop numbers per hectare (2.5 acre) by year.

	Year 1	Year 2	Year 3	Year 4	Year 5	Year 6	Year 7	Year 8	Year 9	Year 10	notes
Banana	252	252	252	252	252	252	252	252	252	252	
Breadfruit	84	84	84	84	84	84	84	84	84	84	
Cacao	378	378	378	378	378	378	378	378	378	378	
Coconut	42	42	42	42	42	42	42	42	42	42	
Kava	1260	1260	1260	840	420	0	0	0	0	0	harvested Years 3–5
Papaya	840	840	840	840	0	0	0	0	0	0	removed in Year 4
Pineapple	10080	10080	10080	10080	0	0	0	0	0	0	removed in Year 4
Taro	1680	0	0	0	0	0	0	0	0	0	harvested Year 1

Table 5.4 Yield estimate for each crop plant Years 1–10 (Elevitch 2011). (1 kg = 2.2 lb)

	Year 1	Year 2	Year 3	Year 4	Year 5	Year 6	Year 7	Year 8	Year 9	Year 10
Banana (fruit kg)	0	40	40	40	40	40	40	40	40	40
Breadfruit (fruit kg)	0	0	10	20	30	40	50	70	90	110
Cacao (whole pod kg)	0	0	5	10	10	10	10	10	10	10
Coconut (nuts count)	0	0	0	0	0	20	40	60	80	80
Kava (root and crown kg)	0	0	4	5	6	0	0	0	0	0
Papaya (fruit kg)	0	10	24	18	0	0	0	0	0	0
Pineapple (fruit kg)	0	1	2	2	0	0	0	0	0	0
Taro (corm kg)	1	0	0	0	0	0	0	0	0	0

For guidance in a local context, existing cost of production analyses for single-commodity plantings can be useful. The single-crop expenses and yields can be adjusted for the crop density of an agroforest. There are several references for calculating production costs for specific Hawai'i crops based on actual expenses or educated guesses for planning purposes.[88]

6 CONCLUSIONS

Breadfruit has been grown for centuries together with other crops in multistory agroforestry throughout the Pacific Islands. Based on those time-tested models, agroforestry is a reduced risk entry point for producers to grow breadfruit with numerous potential benefits.

Table 5.5 Cost of propagation material, planting, and maintenance for each crop (Hawaii estimates).

	Cost of each plant	Planting labor/plant	Planting units	Planting period	Maintenance labor/plant	Maintenance units	Maintenance period
Banana	$5.00	0.1	hr	Year 1	0.25	hr	annual
Breadfruit	$30.00	0.1	hr	Year 1	0.5	hr	annual
Cacao	$20.00	0.1	hr	Year 1	0.25	hr	annual
Coconut	$5.00	0.1	hr	Year 1	0.25	hr	annual
Kava	$5.00	0.1	hr	Year 1	0.1	hr	annual
Papaya	$3.00	0.03	hr	Year 1	0.1	hr	annual
Pineapple	$0.50	0.02	hr	Year 1	0.01	hr	annual
Taro	$1.00	0.01	hr	Year 1	0.01	hr	annual

Table 5.6 Cost of harvest and postharvest specific to each crop (Hawaii estimates).

	Harvest rate	Harvest units	Harvest cost per unit	Harvest cost unit	Postharvest rate	Postharvest units	Postharvest cost per unit	Postharvest cost unit	Postharvest Activity
Banana	120	kg/hr	$0.17	kg	120	kg/hr	$0.17	kg	rinse, sort
Breadfruit	80	kg/hr	$0.25	kg	150	kg/hr	$0.13	kg	rinse, sort
Cacao	100	pod/hr	$0.20	pod	200	kg/hr	$0.10	pod	box
Coconut	60	nuts/hr	$0.33	nut	120	nuts/hr	$0.17	nut	box
Kava	20	kg/hr	$1.00	kg	40	kg/hr	$0.50	kg	rinsing
Papaya	75	kg/hr	$0.27	kg	100	kg/hr	$0.20	kg	rinsing
Pineapple	100	kg/hr	$0.20	kg	200	kg/hr	$0.20	kg	rinsing
Taro	100	kg/hr	$0.20	kg	200	kg/hr	$0.10	kg	rinsing

Table 5.7 Total costs per crop for plant materials, planting, maintenance, harvest, and postharvest (Hawaii estimates).

	Year 1	Year 2	Year 3	Year 4	Year 5	Year 6	Year 7	Year 8	Year 9	Year 10
Banana	$1,764	$4,620	$4,620	$4,620	$4,620	$4,620	$4,620	$4,620	$4,620	$4,620
Breadfruit	$2,688	$840	$1,162	$1,484	$1,806	$2,128	$2,450	$3,094	$3,738	$4,382
Cacao	$8,316	$1,890	$2,457	$3,024	$3,024	$3,024	$3,024	$3,024	$3,024	$3,024
Coconut	$294	$210	$210	$210	$210	$630	$1,050	$1,470	$1,890	$1,890
Kava	$8,820	$2,520	$5,040	$4,830	$4,620	$-	$-	$-	$-	$-
Papaya	$3,024	$5,600	$13,440	$9,520	$-	$-	$-	$-	$-	$-
Pineapple	$9,072	$6,048	$10,080	$10,080	$-	$-	$-	$-	$-	$-
Taro	$2,016	$-	$-	$-	$-	$-	$-	$-	$-	$-
Totals	$35,994	$21,728	$37,009	$33,768	$14,280	$10,402	$11,144	$12,208	$13,272	$13,916

88 CTAHR (n.d.)

Table 5.8 Wholesale crop value per unit (estimated from Hawaii market). Price estimates are based on the local Hawaii certified-organic market, which is higher value than many other markets in the world.

	Unit	Wholesale crop value/kg	Form sold
Banana (fruit)	kg	$1.10	fresh hands, rinsed & sorted
Breadfruit (fruit)	kg	$2.20	fresh mature, rinsed & sorted
Cacao (whole pod)	kg	$1.00	fresh
Coconut (nut)	nut	$2.00	fresh
Kava (root and crown)	kg	$10.00	fresh rinsed & sorted
Papaya (fruit)	kg	$1.10	fresh rinsed & sorted
Pineapple (fruit)	kg	$2.20	fresh rinsed & sorted
Taro (corm)	kg	$2.20	fresh rinsed & sorted

Table 5.9 Estimated income (wholesale value).

	Year 1	Year 2	Year 3	Year 4	Year 5	Year 6	Year 7	Year 8	Year 9	Year 10
Banana	$-	$11,088	$11,088	$11,088	$11,088	$11,088	$11,088	$11,088	$11,088	$11,088
Breadfruit	$-	$-	$1,848	$3,696	$5,544	$7,392	$9,240	$12,936	$16,632	$20,328
Cacao	$-	$-	$1,890	$3,780	$3,780	$3,780	$3,780	$3,780	$3,780	$3,780
Coconut	$-	$-	$-	$-	$-	$1,680	$3,360	$5,040	$6,720	$6,720
Kava	$-	$-	$16,800	$21,000	$25,200	$-	$-	$-	$-	$-
Papaya	$-	$9,240	$22,176	$16,632	$-	$-	$-	$-	$-	$-
Pineapple	$-	$22,176	$44,352	$44,352	$-	$-	$-	$-	$-	$-
Taro	$3,696	$-	$-	$-	$-	$-	$-	$-	$-	$-
Total income	$3,696	$42,504	$98,154	$100,548	$45,612	$23,940	$27,468	$32,844	$38,220	$41,916

Table 5.10 Estimated total expenses and income.

	Year 1	Year 2	Year 3	Year 4	Year 5	Year 6	Year 7	Year 8	Year 9	Year 10
Total expenses	$(64,544)	$(31,378)	$(46,659)	$(43,418)	$(23,930)	$(20,052)	$(20,794)	$(21,858)	$(22,922)	$(23,566)
Total income	$3,696	$42,504	$98,154	$100,548	$45,612	$23,940	$27,468	$32,844	$38,220	$41,916
Cash flow	$(60,848)	$11,126	$51,495	$57,130	$21,682	$3,888	$6,674	$10,986	$15,298	$18,350

Planning is a wise investment, as there are no recipes for agroforestry. Projects are most successful when they are tailored to the site conditions, intended product markets, and personal preferences of the producer.

From a commercial perspective, monocultures tend to have simplified management, as there is only one crop to consider, but they are much more susceptible to pests, weather extremes, market variability, etc. A significant trade-off for an agroforestry production system is the requirement to make management decisions and implement them in real time in order to optimize the performance of all associated crops.

Agroforestry gives producers the opportunity to strengthen their financial position by selecting a crop portfolio that optimizes market opportunities and product line synergies, offers resilience to environmental and economic stressors, and increases total profitability over any single crop.

Subsistence agroforesters have the additional advantage of producing a variety of food, medicinal, and culturally important plants for their own use, helping with home economy.

To maximize profit potential for small farms, it is essential to reach several different markets, including direct retail to consumers and other end users such as chefs, and to wholesale markets. Agroforestry ventures in close proximity to one another might consider collaborating, including through Participatory Guarantee Systems[89] (locally focused quality assurance systems) to supply local and domestic markets. In order to achieve this, a focus on quality from field to market adds value and puts growers at an advantage. Quality begins with design of the agroforest, and extends to care and maintenance, and harvest and postharvest handling.

Financial advantages of a successional agroforest include the production of early yields before breadfruit bears commercial quantities; greater total productivity and profit, if planned well; and applying maintenance efforts to caring for crops rather than fending off weeds.

7 RESOURCES/ORGANIZATIONS

Breadfruit

Breadfruit Institute, National Tropical Botanical Garden: www.breadfruit.org

Ho'oulu ka 'Ulu—Revitalizing Breadfruit: www.breadfruit.info

Agroforestry

Agroforestry Net: www.agroforestry.org

World Agroforestry Center: www.worldagroforestrycentre.org

Organic agriculture

Regenerative Organic Certification: www.regenorganic.org

Western SARE: www.westernsare.org

ECHO: www.echonet.org

Rodale Institute: rodaleinstitute.org

Trees for the Future: www.trees.org

State of Hawaii Department of Agriculture: hdoa.hawaii.gov

8 REFERENCES

Adeleke, R.O., and O.A. Abiobun. 2010. Nutritional composition of breadnut seeds (*Artocarpus camansi*). *African J Agricultural Research* 5(11): 1273–1276.

Altieri, M.A. 1995. *Agroecology: the science of sustainable agriculture.* CRC Press.

Altieri, M.A. 2007. Fatal harvest: old and new dimensions of the ecological tragedy of modern agriculture. *JBAPA, 30–31,* 189–213.

Aurore, G., J. Nacitas, B. Parfait, and L. Fahrasmane. 2014. Seeded breadfruit naturalized in the Caribbean is not a seeded variety of *Artocarpus altilis. Genetic Resources & Crop Evolution* 61: 901–907.

Bell, J., and M. Taylor. 2015. *Building Climate-Resilient Food Systems for Pacific Islands.* WorldFish.

BFI. 2016. *How to Dry and Grind Breadfruit into Flour.* Breadfruit Institute, National Tropical Botanical Garden. Kalaheo, Hawaii. https://ntbg.org/breadfruit/resources

Bornhorst, H. 2012. *How to Plant a Tree of Life.* Breadfruit Institute, Kalaheo, Hawaii.

Cho, H.K., and A. Koyama. 1997. *Korean Natural Farming: Indigenous microorganisms and vital power of crop/livestock.* Korean Natural Farming.

Clarke, W.C. and Thaman, R.R. 1993. *Agroforestry in the Pacific Islands: systems for sustainability.* United Nations University Press.

Coronel, R.E. 1983. Rimas and kamansi. In *Promising fruits of the Philippines.* Pp. 379-396. College of Agriculture, University of the Philippines at Los Baños.

CTAHR (n.d.). CTAHR Farm Food Safety: Good Agricultural Practices Education. University of Hawaii College of Tropical Agriculture and Human Resources, Manoa, Hawaii. http://manoa.hawaii.edu/ctahr/farmfoodsafety/

CTI. 2012. *Breadfruit Flour. Tools that Empower Communities.* Compatible Technology International. http://momedyblog.com/our-tools/emerging-technologies/breadfruit-tools.html

Elevitch, C.R. 2011. *Specialty Crops for Pacific Islands.* Permanent Agriculture Resources, Holualoa, Hawaii. www.specialtycrops.info

---

89 IFOAM 2017

Elevitch, C.R. 2015. Getting started with food-producing agroforestry landscapes in the Pacific. In Elevitch, C.R. (Ed.). *Food-Producing Agroforestry Landscapes of the Pacific.* Permanent Agriculture Resources (PAR), Holualoa, Hawaii. www.agroforestry.org

Elevitch, C., and K. Love. 2013. *Adding Value to Locally Grown Crops in Hawai'i: A Guide for Small Farm Enterprise Innovation.* Permanent Agriculture Resources, Holualoa, Hawaii. www.valueadded.info

Elevitch, C., D. Ragone, and I. Cole. 2014. *Breadfruit Production Guide: Recommended practices for growing, harvesting, and handling (2nd Edition).* Breadfruit Institute of the National Tropical Botanical Garden, Kalaheo, Hawaii and Hawaii Homegrown Food Network, Holualoa, Hawaii. www.breadfruit.org and www.breadfruit.info

Elevitch, C., G. Behling, M. Constantinides, and J.B. Friday. 2015. Grower's guide to Pacific Island agroforestry systems, information resources, and public assistance programs. pp. 262–316. In Elevitch, C.R. (Ed.). *Food-Producing Agroforestry Landscapes of the Pacific.* Permanent Agriculture Resources (PAR), Holualoa, Hawaii. www.agroforestry.org

Evans, D.O., R.J. Joy, and C.L. Chia. 1988. *Cover Crops for Orchards in Hawaii.* Hawaii Institute of Tropical Agriculture and Human Resources, Honolulu, Hawaii.

Fleming, K., V. Easton-Smith, and H.C. Bittenbender. 2009. The Economics of Cacao Production in Kona. AgriBusiness AB-1712. University of Hawai'i, Honolulu. http://www.ctahr.hawaii.edu/oc/freepubs/pdf/AB-17.pdf

Fownes, J.H., and W.C. Raynor. 1993. Seasonality and yield of breadfruit cultivars in the indigenous agroforestry system of Pohnpei, Federated States of Micronesia. *Tropical Agriculture (Trinidad)* 70(2): 103–109.

Giambelluca, T.W., Q. Chen, A.G. Frazier, J.P. Price, Y.-L. Chen, P.-S. Chu, J.K. Eischeid, and D.M. Delparte. 2013. Online Rainfall Atlas of Hawai'i. *Bulletin American Meteorology Society.* 94, 313–316.

Godsey, L.D. 2010. *Economic Budgeting for Agroforestry Practices.* University of Missouri Center for Agroforestry, Columbia.

Higa, T., and G.N. Wididana. 1991. The concept and theories of effective microorganisms. In: *Proceedings of the First International Conference on Kyusei Nature Farming.* pp. 118–124. US Department of Agriculture, Washington, DC.

IFOAM. 2017. *How Governments Can Support Participatory Guarantee System (PGS).* IFOAM–Organics International, Bonn, Germany.

Jones, A.M.P., S.J. Murch, and D. Ragone. 2010. Diversity of breadfruit (*Artocarpus altilis*, Moraceae) seasonality: A resource for year-round nutrition. *Economic Botany* 64(4): 340–351.

Jones, A.M.P., D. Ragone, K. Aiona, W.A. Lane, and S.J. Murch. 2011. Nutritional and morphological diversity of breadfruit (*Artocarpus*, Moraceae): identification of elite cultivars for food security. *Journal of Food Composition & Analysis* 24(8): 1091–1102.

Jones, A.M.P., R. Baker, D. Ragone, and S J. Murch. 2013. Identification of pro-vitamin A carotenoid-rich cultivars of breadfruit (*Artocarpus*, Moraceae). *Journal of Food Composition & Analysis* 31(1): 51–61.

Kumar, B.M., and P.K. Nair. (Eds.). 2007. *Tropical Homegardens: A time-tested example of sustainable agroforestry* (Vol. 3). Springer Science & Business Media.

Lau, J-W. 2017. Plant Parasitic Nematodes Associated with Breadfruit, *Artocarpus altilis* (Parkinson) Fosberg. Master's Thesis. Department of Tropical Plant and Environmental Protection Science, University of Hawaii at Manoa, Honolulu.

Leakey, R.R.B. 1999. Agroforestry for biodiversity in farming systems. *Biodiversity in Agroecosystems,* 127–145.

Leakey, R.R.B. 2014. The role of trees in agroecology and sustainable agriculture in the tropics. *Annual Review of Phytopathology,* 52(1), 113–133.

Leakey, R.R.B. 2017. *Multifunctional Agriculture: Achieving Sustainable Development in Africa.* Academic Press.

Lincoln, N. and T. Lagefoged. 2014. Agroecology of pre-contact Hawaiian dryland farming: the spatial extent, yield and social impact of Hawaiian breadfruit groves in Kona, Hawai'i. *Journal of Archaeological Science* 49: 192–202.

Liu, Y., A.M.P. Jones, S.J. Murch, and D. Ragone. 2014. Crop productivity, yield and seasonality of breadfruit (*Artocarpus* spp.) Moraceae. *Fruits* 69: 345–361.

Liu, Y., D. Ragone, and S.J. Murch. 2015. Breadfruit (*Artocarpus altilis*): a source of high-quality protein for food security and novel food products. *Amino Acids* 47(4): 847–856.

Lucas, M.P., and D. Ragone. 2012. Will breadfruit solve the world hunger crisis? New developments in an innovative food crop. *ArcNews* Summer 6–8.

McGregor, A. and K. Stice. 2018. *Breadfruit Market and Marketing of Pacific Island Breadfruit with a Focus on Fiji & Samoa*. Pacific Island Farmers Organisation Network. Suva, Fiji.

McLaurin, W.J., and W. Reeves. 2014. *How to Convert an Inorganic Fertilizer Recommendation to an Organic One*. University of Georgia Extension Circular 853. Athens, GA.

Mead, R., and R.W. Willey. 1980. The concept of a 'land equivalent ratio' and advantages in yields from intercropping. *Experimental Agriculture*, 16(03), 217–228. http://dx.doi.org/10.1017/S0014479700010978

Meilleur, B.A., R.R. Jones, C.A. Titchenal, and A.S. Huang. 2004. *Hawaiian Breadfruit: Ethnobotany, nutrition, and human ecology*. University of Hawaii Press, Honolulu, Hawaii.

NARI, 2010. Breadfruit flour. In O. Homenauth (Ed.), *Agroprocessing Manual*. 29. The Guyana Ministry of Agriculture Agro Advertising & Marketing Service, Georgetown.

NWC (Natures Way Cooperative). 2005. *A Manual for the Growing and Marketing of Breadfruit for Export*. Natures Way Cooperative, Ltd., Fiji.

Nelson, S.C. 2006. *Poly and Monocultures: the Good, the Bad and the Ugly*. Agroforestry Net, Holualoa, Hawaii.

NSF International. 2017. Recommended Framework for Regenerative Organic Certification. http://standards.nsf.org/apps/group_public/document.php?document_id=39305

Pachauri, R.K., M.R. Allen, V.R. Barros, J. Broome, W. Cramer, R. Christ, et al. 2014. Climate change 2014: synthesis report. Contribution of Working Groups I, II and III to the fifth assessment report of the Intergovernmental Panel on Climate Change. IPCC. https://epic.awi.de/37530/

Produce Safety Alliance. (n.d.). https://producesafetyalliance.cornell.edu/

Pumariño, L., G.W. Sileshi, S. Gripenberg, R. Kaartinen, E. Barrios, M.N. Muchane, M. Jonsson. 2015. Effects of agroforestry on pest, disease and weed control: A meta-analysis. *Basic and Applied Ecology*, 16(7), 573–582.

Radovich, T., and N. Arancon. 2011. *Tea Time in the Tropics: A Handbook for Compost Tea Production and Use*. College of Tropical Agriculture and Human Resources, University of Hawaii.

Ragone, D. 1997. *Breadfruit. Artocarpus altilis (Parkinson) Fosberg. Promoting the conservation and use of underutilized and neglected crops*. 10. International Plant Genetic Resources Institute, Rome, Italy.

Ragone, D. 2006. *Artocarpus altilis* (Breadfruit). pp. 85–100. In Elevitch, C.R. (Ed.). *Traditional Trees of Pacific Islands: Their culture, environment, and use*. Permanent Agriculture Resources (PAR), Holualoa, Hawaii. http://www.traditionaltree.org

Ragone, D. 2006. *Artocarpus camansi* (breadnut). pp. 85–100. In Elevitch, C.R. (Ed.), *Traditional Trees of Pacific Islands: Their culture, environment, and use*. Permanent Agriculture Resources (PAR), Holualoa, Hawaii. http://www.traditionaltree.org

Ragone, D. and H.I. Manner. 2006. *Artocarpus mariannensis* (Dugdug). pp. 127–138. In Elevitch, C.R. (Ed.), *Traditional Trees of Pacific Islands: Their culture, environment, and use*. Permanent Agriculture Resources (PAR), Holualoa, Hawaii. http://www.traditionaltree.org

Ragone D. 2008. Regeneration guidelines: breadfruit. In Dulloo M.E., Thormann I., Jorge M.A. and Hanson J., (Eds.). *Crop Specific Regeneration Guidelines* [CD-ROM]. CGIAR Systemwide Genetic Resource Programme, Rome, Italy. 7 pp. https://cropgenebank.sgrp.cgiar.org/index.php/crops-mainmenu-367/other-crops-regeneration-guidelines-mainmenu-290/breadfruit-mainmenu-398

Ragone, D. 2011. Farm and forestry production and marketing profile for breadfruit (*Artocarpus altilis*). pp. 127-138. In Elevitch, C.R. (Ed.), *Specialty Crops for Pacific Island Agroforestry*. Permanent Agriculture Resources (PAR), Holualoa, Hawaii. http://specialtycrops.info

Ragone, D., and C.G. Cavaletto. 2006. Sensory evaluation of fruit quality and nutritional composition of 20 breadfruit (*Artocarpus*, Moraceae) cultivars. *Economic Botany* 60(4): 335–346.

Ragone, D., and W.C. Raynor. 2009. Breadfruit and its traditional cultivation and use on Pohnpei. p. 63–88. In M.J. Balick (Ed.), *Ethnobotany of Pohnpei: plants, people, and island culture*. University of Hawaii Press & New York Botanical Garden Press, NY.

Ragone, D., C.R. Elevitch, D. Shapiro, and A. Dean. (Eds.) 2012. *Hoʻoulu ka ʻUlu Cookbook: Breadfruit tips, techniques, and Hawaiʻi's favorite home recipes*. Breadfruit Institute of the National Tropical Botanical Garden, Kalaheo, Hawaii and Hawaiʻi Homegrown Food Network, Holualoa, Hawaii. http://breadfruit.org

Ragone, D., C. Elevitch and A. Dean. 2016. Revitalizing breadfruit in Hawaii—A model for encouraging the cultivation and use of breadfruit in the tropics. *Tropical Agriculture (Trinidad)*, 213–224.

Redfern, T.N. 2007. Breadfruit improvement activities in Kiribati. *Acta Horticulturae* 757:93–99.

Roberts-Nkrumah, L.B. 2005. Fruit and seed yields in chataigne (*Artocarpus camansi* Blanco) in Trinidad and Tobago. *Fruits*, 60(6), 387–393.

Roberts-Nkrumah, L.B. 2015. *Breadfruit and Breadnut Orchard Establishment and Management: A manual for commercial production*. Food and Agriculture Organization of the United Nations.

Roberts-Nkrumah, L.B., and E.J. Duncan (Eds). 2016. *Proceedings of the International Breadfruit Conference—Commercialising Breadfruit for Food and Nutrition Security*. Republic of Trinidad and Tobago: The University of the West Indies.

Rodale Institute. 2014. Regenerative Organic Agriculture and Climate Change. Rodale Institute. http://rodaleinstitute.org/assets/WhitePaper.pdf

SOAP (Sustainable and Organic Agriculture Program). 2018. Covering New Ground: Tropical Cover Crops for Improving Soil Quality. https://www.ctahr.hawaii.edu/sustainag/database.asp

Toensmeier, E. 2016. *The Carbon Farming Solution: A global toolkit of perennial crops and regenerative agriculture practices for climate change mitigation and food security*. Chelsea Green Publishing, Hartford, Vermont.

Thomson, L.A.J. and R.R. Thaman. 2016. Native forests, plantation forests and trees outside forests: their vulnerability and roles in mitigating and building resilience to climate change. pp 383–446 In Taylor, M.,

A. McGregor, and B. Dawson (Eds). *Vulnerability of Pacific Island agriculture and forestry to climate change*. Pacific Community, Noumea.

Tora, L.D., V. Lebot, and A.M. McGregor. 2014. Planting breadfruit orchards as a climate change adaptation strategy for the Pacific Islands. In *XXIX International Horticultural Congress on Horticulture: Sustaining lives, livelihoods and landscapes (IHC2014): 1128* (pp. 55–66). http://www.actahort.org/books/1128/1128_8.htm

Torquebiau, E.F. 2000. A renewed perspective on agroforestry concepts and classification. *Comptes Rendus de l'Académie Des Sciences - Series III - Sciences de La Vie*, 323(11), 1009–1017.

TTFF. 2016. *Factory in a box and breadfruit flour production*. Trees That Feed Foundation. Winnetka, Illinois.

Turi, C., Y. Liu, D. Ragone, and S.J. Murch. 2015. Breadfruit (*Artocarpus altilis* and hybrids): A traditional crop with the potential to prevent hunger and mitigate diabetes in Oceania. *Trends in Food Science & Technology* 45(2): 264–272.

USDA FDA CFSAN/Office of Food Additive Safety. 2016. Agency Response Letter GRAS Notice No. GRN 000596. https://www.fda.gov/Food/IngredientsPackagingLabeling/GRAS/NoticeInventory/ucm495765.htm

Webster, S.A. 2006. *The Breadfruit in Jamaica: A commercial & horticultural perspective*. Seymour Webster, Portland, Jamaica.

Wilkinson, K.M., and C.R. Elevitch. 2000. Integrating understory crops with tree crops: an introductory guide for Pacific Islands. pp. 99–120. In Elevitch, C.R., and K.M. Wilkinson (Eds). *Agroforestry Guides for Pacific Islands*. Permanent Agriculture Resources, Holualoa, Hawaii.

Williams, K., and N. Badrie. 2005. Nutritional composition and sensory acceptance of boiled breadnut (*Artocarpus camansi* Blanco) seeds. *Journal of Food Technology* 3(4): 546–551.

Yeomans, A.J. 2005. *Priority One*. Keyline Publishing Co. Australia.

Zerega, N.J.C., D. Ragone, and T.J. Motley. 2004. Complex origins of breadfruit (*Artocarpus altilis*, Moraceae): implications for human migrations in Oceania. *American Journal of Botany* 91: 760–766.

Notes